TURN BUT A STONE

The angels keep their ancient places:–
Turn but a stone, and start a wing!
'Tis ye, 'tis your estrangèd faces,
That miss the many-splendoured thing.

Francis Thompson, from *The Kingdom of God*.

TURN BUT
A STONE

Edmund Banyard

*A collection of meditations and prayers
based on the Lectionary*

NCEC

Other books by Edmund Banyard published by NCEC.

Fistful of Fivers
The Flame
The Maker of Things
(with Graham Bishop-Hunt)

Cover design:
Peggy Chapman

Published by:
National Christian Education Council
Robert Denholm House
Nutfield
Redhill RH1 4HW

British Library Cataloguing-in-Publication Data:
Banyard, Edmund
  Turn But a Stone
  I. Title
  242

ISBN 0-7197-0785-4

First published 1992
© Edmund Banyard 1992

Typeset by One and A Half Graphics, Redhill, Surrey.
Printed and bound by BPCC–AUP Aberdeen Ltd.

Contents

9th before Christmas — Source Of All That Is / God Is Not Like Me

8th before Christmas — The Knowledge That Is Ignorance / Stirrings Of Anger / Messages Of Hope / A Working Partnership

7th before Christmas — God's People? Why Abraham? / We Pray For A Miracle

6th before Christmas — At The Burning Bush / Lord, Set Us Free

5th before Christmas — If Only I Could Have a Subscription Account / 'Then you hear God Thinking'

Advent 1 — Are You Listening? / God's Rescue Operation

Advent 2 — He Has Sent Me / The Holy Scriptures

Advent 3 — Strange Comfort / Come, Lord Jesus

Advent 4 — Judgement / Teach Us To Love

Christmas — The Word / The Word Became Flesh / No Room At The Inn / The Significance Of Simple Things.

Next before Epiphany — Old Man And Infant / Mother And Son

Epiphany — I Would Be Wise / Abba Father

1st after Epiphany — The Buck Stops Here / The Baptism Of Repentance

2nd after Epiphany — No Easy Calling / The Voice Of The Lord

3rd after Epiphany — Strange Miracle / The Surprising Kingdom

4th after Epiphany — Our Love And Our Perplexity / The Freedom Of The Children Of God

5th after Epiphany — Look For The Light / The Hope In Christ (An Intercession)

6th after Epiphany — The God Given Sabbath / Beyond All Dreams Of Avarice

9th before Easter — No Easy Lessons / Ears To Hear

8th before Easter — The Paralysed Man / The Leper

7th before Easter — They Ate And Were Satisfied / Only Comprehended By Love

6th before Easter — Angel Or Tempter? / Facing Temptation (An Intercession)

5th before Easter — To Fight Or Not To Fight? / This Is No War Game

4th before Easter — Are We To Put All At Risk? / The Call To The Unknown

3rd before Easter — Truth Is Frightening / The Serving Community

2nd before Easter — No Easy Road / Triumph Through Suffering (An Intercession)

Palm Sunday — The Foolishness Which Confounds Our Wisdom / Holy Week Meditation

Maundy Thursday — The One Who Serves

Good Friday — At The Cross / Mary Magdalene – Friday

Easter Day — Mary Magdalene – Easter Morning

1st after Easter — A Gloriously Inverted View Of Life

1st after Easter — Pull Back The Bolts / It Was The Lord!

Contents

2nd after Easter	This I Believe Even New Life Has Its Problems	9th after Pentecost	Love, The Ultimate Weapon To Be Of The Kingdom
3rd after Easter	The Life We Seek Feed My Sheep	10th after Pentecost	At The Lord's Table The Open Door Of The Church
4th after Easter	The Pilgrim Way Nine Gifts In One	11th after Pentecost	Like A Child Nothing Is Greater Than Love
5th after Easter	Down But Not Out O Crucified And Risen Lord (An Easter hymn)	12th after Pentecost	Fools Gold? Help Us As We Hesitate
6th after Easter (Ascension)	The Risen Lord (An Intercession) Ascension	13th after Pentecost	And Afterwards? Our Greater Need
Pentecost	The Real Babel Life In The Spirit (An Intercession)	14th after Pentecost	Make Us Aware Prayer Of A Wayfarer
1st after Pentecost (Trinity)	Too Small A Vision? Too Large A Task?	15th after Pentecost	Ready To Be Disciples The Unity Of The Church
2nd after Pentecost	All Things In Common Also Your Children	16th after Pentecost	The Medium Is The Message? Why This Waste?
3rd after Pentecost	No Other Name Prayer In Time Of Difficulty	17th after Pentecost	What Does Love Demand? Prayer For The Family (An Intercession)
4th after Pentecost	The Inner Spring Of The Water Of Life When The Springs Of My Life Run Dry	18th after Pentecost	You Won't Believe It! So Much Yet So Little
5th after Pentecost	Prayer For The City Freedom	19th after Pentecost	That We May See The Glory Renewal
6th after Pentecost	Prayer Of A Sinner The Human Face Of The Almighty	20th after Pentecost	Pay Caesar What Is Due To Caesar Pay Caesar What Is Due To Caesar (An Intercession)
7th after Pentecost	Love In Action. Before The Harvest	21st after Pentecost	In A Time Of Crisis (An Intercession) The Buried Talent
8th after Pentecost	Fools For The Lord The Source Of Peace (An Intercession)	22nd after Pentecost	Losing And Winning By What Authority?
		Last after Pentecost	The Race The Eternal Kingdom
		Harvest	The Good Earth Blessed Be The Name Of The Lord

Preface

The meditations, lyrics, and prayers in *Turn But a Stone* have been gradually written, modified, rewritten and modified again over many years. They have now been brought together within the framework of the Christian Year following the lectionary, *(JLG2)*, of the Joint Liturgical Group.

This lectionary, covering as it does a four year cycle, offers a wide choice of passages, sometimes embarrassingly so, as in the eighth week before Christmas where both the Fall and the Flood cry out to be used. Instead of picking up all possible themes, I have deliberately selected those which spoke most strongly to me. The Liturgical calendar has provided a useful and stimulating framework, but it is not a straightjacket, and the outline and the indices are intended to simplify the using of material at other times.

More often than not the first person plural has been used, partly because the material can and has been used corporately, but also because in a very real sense we can never pray alone. That is, all true prayer must surely have some awareness of the fact that we live our lives in community where the simplest actions can affect a wide range of people.

Even more, Christians are called to be part of the Body of Christ, whose love embraces the whole world, which means that our living and praying has of necessity to be interwoven with the other members of that body.

Some pieces have been published previously, particularly in *All Year Round,* (CCBI). Where they are extracted from a larger work the source is indicated.

Edmund Banyard
Diss, Norfolk
1992

Abbreviations and Acknowledgements

We are grateful for permission to quote from the following Bible versions:

AV Authorized Version

NEB New English Bible

REB Revised English Bible

RSV Revised Standard Version

The compiler and publishers express thanks for permission to use copyright items. Every effort has been made to trace copyright owners but if any rights have been inadvertently overlooked, the necessary correction will gladly be made in subsequent editions.

Page

71 Dietrich Bonhoeffer from *Letters and Papers from Prison*, The Enlarged Edition (© 1971), used with permission of SCM Press 1971

21 J. Bronowski from *The Ascent of Man* reproduced with permission of BBC Enterprises Ltd

The copyright for the following items is held by Stainer and Bell Ltd and they are used with permission.

20 'Lord it would be so much easier' first appeared in the anthology *Prophets in Action.*

32 'I may leave the Bible neatly shelved' first appeared in the anthology *News Extra.*

79 The two speeches by Mary Magdalene are from the play *One Friday in Eternity.*

91 'O crucified and risen Lord' and

149 'O Lord of the Kingdom' first appeared in *All Year Round* 1987.

The copyright for the following items remains with the author.

34 'Beggarman' is from the musical play *George* published by Radius.

156 'O the grain in the hand' is from the musical play *The Alien* published by Radius.

48 'It was unobtrusive the Coming' is from the Christmas script The Coming which was reproduced in *All Year Round* (1990).

114 'Fools for the Lord' and

122 'Can you imagine just one thing' are from the musical play *Ragman* based on Paul's experience at Ephesus, produced at the Westminster Theatre 1980

Source Of All That Is

9th before Christmas

In the beginning God created the heavens and the earth.
Genesis 1.1 REB

The heavens tell out the glory of God, heaven's vault makes known his
*   handiwork.*
One day speaks to another, night to night imparts knowledge,
and this without speech or language or sound of any voice.
Their sign shines forth on all the earth, their message to the ends of the world.
Psalm 19.1–4 REB

We worship you the ever living God,
The WORD, spoken before time was,
The WORD, eternally speaking in the present,
Creator, source of all that is.

We praise you for light,
revealing shape, colour and texture.

We praise you for the rhythms within the universe
giving wakefulness and sleep,
night and day,
seedtime and harvest.

We praise you for life-giving water
everlastingly recycled,
for the atmosphere we breathe
and for the earth beneath our feet.

We praise you for the rich diversity
of living creatures,
for the miracle of being human,
animal, yet so much more than animal.

Forgive us when we go blindly through the world.
Forgive us when we spoil, waste and abuse your gifts.
Forgive us when we forget that we walk on holy ground
and renew our sense of awe, wonder, and sheer delight
in the riches of your creation.

You are worthy, O Lord our God, to receive glory and honour and power, because
you created all things; by your will they were created and have their being!
Revelation 4.11 REB

God is not like me

**9th
before
Christmas**

Let us make human beings in our image, after our likeness.
Genesis 1.26 REB

*The Lord God formed a human being from the dust of the ground and breathed
into his nostrils the breath of life.*
Genesis 2.7 REB

God is not like me.
I have not moulded him in my image,
but he has made me in his.
The image is twisted,
distorted,
a ghastly caricature
from a hall of mirrors;
yet,
marred as it is,
the image of God is there.

I am no mere accident.
I have been willed into being
within a purposeful creation;
and yet-
    Who am I?
    What am I?

I read that I am frail as dust
and I know this is true.
I may dream and scheme and plan
but shall I live to do what I have dreamed?

I am common clay,
yet common clay touched by the breath of God;
within this frail shell
dwells something of eternity.

To know myself
I must learn from my Creator.
To find myself
I must seek for God.

    **Forgive me, my Lord, my Maker,
    that I have so distorted
    the image which I bear.
    Remake me, I pray,
    breathe fresh life into me,
    that I may more truly
    reflect your glory in the world.**

The Knowledge That Is Ignorance

8th before Christmas

The fallen state of humanity is described in a story. The man and the woman are tempted to eat forbidden fruit with the words, 'Of course you will not die - your eyes will be opened and you will be like gods knowing both good and evil.'

Genesis 3.4 – 5 NEB

You are the source
of all knowledge and truth;
you are our Maker,
and 'good'
is what you are.
When we claim the right
to name our own good and our own evil
disintegration,
fragmentation
has already begun.
Before we realise what has happened
barriers have grown,
differences have been magnified;
differences of sex, race, creed,
colour, language, culture.
From the hub of our home-made universe
we view our neighbours with fear,
suspicion, hostility.
Our vaunted rights
have become our prisons,
we are estranged from You
and estranged from one another.

**Almighty God,
by whatever name we call upon you,
you are One,
Lord of all peoples.
Save us from our self-made isolation.
Save us from the sight that is blindness
and the knowledge that is ignorance
and lead us we pray into the way of life.**

God loved the world so much that he gave his only Son, that everyone who has faith in him may not die but have eternal life. It was not to judge the world that God sent his son into the world, but that through him the world might be saved.

John 3.16 – 17 NEB

11

Stirrings Of Anger

8th
before
Christmas

The Lord received Abel and his gift with favour; but Cain and his gift he did not receive. Cain was very angry and his face fell.

Genesis 4.4 – 5 NEB

For the message you have heard from the beginning is this: that we should love one another; unlike Cain, who was a child of the evil one and murdered his brother.

1 John 3.11 – 12 NEB

Beneath an outward calm
I too have felt stirrings of anger
when others were preferred before me,
received more notice,
or had greater success.
Instinctively
I have sought to defend my status;
all those little privileges
I have inherited
or earned;
all those things
which together
mark me out,
prove I am different . . .

> Help me, my Saviour,
> when the blood of Cain
> flows hot in my veins,
> when it is at my door
> that the demon crouches;
> help me to wrestle
> with this enemy.
> Deliver me from envy,
> from false pride,
> and all else that would
> destroy me from within,
> for I cannot be at peace
> with my brothers and sisters
> until I am at peace
> with myself.

Messages Of Hope

When I bring clouds over the earth, the rainbow will appear in the clouds.

Genesis 9.14 REB

Alarm bells ring!
Sirens sound!
Storm cones are hoisted!
Everywhere, warnings of disaster:
- By wasting of the earth's resources.
- By over-population.
- By pollution.
- By anarchy.
- By nuclear holocaust.
- By earthquake.
- By cold.
- By heat.
- By drought.
- By flood . . .

And across the ages
come images,
messengers of hope:
- A frail ark riding on the flood.
- A dove with an olive leaf.
- A rainbow.

> Lord of all that is,
> all that has been,
> and all that is to come;
> you are the beginning and the end.
> A man, a woman, a people, a church,
> the noblest of our dreams,
> all these will pass;
> but your grand design will not be overthrown.
> You make disasters source of new beginnings;
> death but the prelude to resurrection.
> We hear the cries of doom
> but live by faith.

A Working Partnership

8th before Christmas

I am now establishing my covenant with you and with your descendants after you.

Genesis 9.9 REB

Lord of the ages,
what can we say in response to your initiative,
for you,
the source of all that is,
offer to us a working partnership?

You reach out to us in care,
but it is for us to build the ark
against the time of flood,
and it is for us
to stop the passengers
devouring one another.

You have given us a fruitful earth
and changing seasons,
but we must build our shelters
from the elements,
plant seed
and labour for the harvest.

You give us the earth
and the vision of life as it might be,
but it is for us
to strive to make that vision reality
and to feel with you
the pain of covenant rejected.

When we have done all
and the flood still threatens to engulf us,
you remain faithful to your covenant;
You are still the God
who breaks into life as rescuer.
You are the God
we may trust to the end of time.

God's People? Why Abraham?

7th before Christmas

I shall bless you and make your name so great that it will be used in blessings.
Genesis 12.2 REB

Why should one be called
and not another,
if you are indeed
the God of all peoples?
Why are some singled out
for your favours?
Why Abraham?

Abraham was called
not to have
but to give;
not to acquire status
but to serve;
not to be elite,
but to be the first true universalist.
Abraham was called
to leave the known for the unknown;
to be a wanderer in the land of promise;
to have no foothold but a burial place.
Called to be blessed;
much more he was called
to be a blessing.

Is this then what 'calling' means.
To be a people on the move,
not clinging to the tried,
the safe,
the known;
but travelling,
responding to a half-heard voice?

To be a people on the move
whose goal
is not their own salvation
into some exclusive heavenly club,
but the fulfilment of your purposes
for all humanity,
the salvation of the world?

We Pray For A Miracle

7th before Christmas

He pitched his tent . . . He built there an altar.

Genesis 12.8 REB

Father, we fear that we often
come to you for the wrong reasons,
asking you to preserve the little corner
we have made our own.
We pray for our health,
our homes,
our jobs,
our family,
our nation . . .
We pray for all we have
and know
to be preserved,
as if you were
the great underwriter in the sky
and prayer the premium you require
to save our policy from lapsing.

Forgive us that we are over-anxious
about the very things
you tell us not to be anxious about
and that we are not nearly so concerned
as we should be
about the work to which you call us.

Forgive us our lack
of understanding,
of vision,
of faith.
Teach us to listen
for the word you have for us
and make us more ready to venture
where you would have us go.

Lord, we pray for a miracle,
take the stony soil
of these lives of ours
and from it make us
children unto Abraham.

At The Burning Bush

6th before Christmas

There an angel of the Lord appeared to him as a fire blazing out from a bush.
Exodus 3.2 REB

In the long hours spent in the wilderness it would be surprising if the passion for justice which Moses had shown as a young man didn't lead him to ask himself, 'If there is a God, why doesn't he intervene?' Suddenly he heard the answer.

In the all-too familiar
wilderness,
endlessly traversed
in search of pasture,
the God of his fathers
met with him.
So the wilderness
became holy ground,
and he was directed
to another task;
another wilderness.

What would happen
to us, Lord,
if familiar places
were suddenly
to be transformed
into holy ground?
Would the pattern of our living
be shattered?
Would our present ideas
of what it means
to follow you
be revealed as illusions?

I would stand
before the burning bush
and see the glory of God
blazing in life's wilderness.
I would wonder,
worship,
and be still.

At The Burning Bush

But what if I
should hear that voice
practical,
earthy,
specific,
speaking to me?

What if God should say,
'I have heard,
I will save,
now you must hear
and go
and be the instrument
of my salvation'.

I want to stand
and see the glory of God,
to wonder,
worship
and be still . . .
but what if God says, 'Go!'?

Lord, Set Us Free

6th before Christmas

Come, I shall send you to Pharaoh, and you are to bring my people out of Egypt.
Exodus 3.10 REB

Saviour Lord,
if ever we are to be the means
of bringing freedom to others
we shall firstly need
to be set free ourselves.

Release us, we pray,
from the pride,
the greed,
and all the self-centred
and defensive attitudes
that bind us.
Above all
free us from the illusion
that we can somehow save ourselves.

Make us free
as only you can;
that we may be passionately concerned
for the freedom of others.
Let us not rest content
while we have sisters and brothers
enslaved by poverty, hunger,
ignorance, oppression;
who have no homeland, no rights
and little hope.

Lord, give us the will
and the stamina
to fight your battles,
to refuse to be put off by easy solutions
that are no solutions,
and to continue steadfastly
in the work to which you call us
all the days of our life.

If Only I Could Have A Subscription Account

5th before Christmas

One thing you lack . . . come and follow me.

Mark 10.21 REB

Lord, it would be so much easier
if I could have a subscription account;
pay you regularly
by direct debit,
and know that I could do
just what I liked
with the rest of my living.

I grumble about the tax-man,
who doesn't?
But when he's fixed his share
the rest is mine,
and he doesn't want to know about it
until the next returns are due.

But you!
You ask for nothing
and yet you ask for everything!
It's not enough for you
that I give generously to the church
and subscribe to charities.
If I gave away my last penny
you still wouldn't be satisfied.
You probe my attitudes,
my aims,
my ideals,
my secret hopes and fears.

Lord, it would be so much easier
if I could have a subscription account,
pay you regularly
and know that I could do
just what I liked
with the rest of my living.
But you are not content with my money,
not even with a share of my time,
you won't let me get away with
a subscription account,
you want
ME!

From *Prophets in Action*

'Then You Hear God Thinking'

'My task is to bear witness to the truth. For this I was born; for this I came into the world . . . ' Pilate said, 'What is truth?'

John 18.38 REB

Einstein was full of humanity, pity, a sense of enormous sympathy. His vision of nature herself was that of a human being in the presence of something god-like, and that is what he always said about nature. He was fond of talking about God. Einstein was a man who could ask immensely simple questions. And what his life showed, and his work, is that when the answers are simple too, then you hear God thinking.

J.Bronowski. From *The Ascent of Man*

Father,
why are we such restless creatures,
so often longing for something different,
so often looking for a happiness
beyond our present experience?

Is this restlessness evil
or is it a gift?
Might it come from you?
Could it be a divine discontent
which will never be satisfied
until we have discovered
the inner meaning of our lives?

Help us to ask the right questions
of our world
and of our own daily living;
and save us from being content
with inadequate answers.
Teach us the humility
of the truly wise
who know that the nearer they come
to the heart of truth
the nearer they will be
to you.

Are You Listening?

4th before Christmas (Advent 1)

It is high time for you to wake out of sleep.

Romans 13.11 REB

Quiet puss!
Someone's at the door,
we must be very still!

Good,
they've gone.
It would only be
the woman from the Welfare,
someone selling flags or brushes,
or wanting to ask questions
for one of those surveys.

We would know,
you and I,
if it was anyone who mattered,
wouldn't we?
But of course
no one who mattered
would come here.

Shush!
That's more footsteps
. . .

They've gone again.

Yes puss,
life is lonely,
just you and me;
day after day
we sit
and the hours
can be very long.

Just you and me,
and no one
ever calls . . .

God's Rescue Operation

4th before Christmas (Advent 1)

How beautiful on the mountains are the feet of the herald, the bringer of good news, announcing deliverance.

Isaiah 52.7 REB

The whole world from end to end shall see the deliverance wrought by our God.
Isaiah 52.10 REB

Can news ever be good for everybody?
Can one win
without another losing?
Can one eat
without another going hungry?
Can one grow richer
without another growing poorer?
Surely if it is good for the warder
it is bad for the prisoner;
good for the Arab,
bad for the Jew;
good for the establishment,
bad for the revolution?

But what if all are losers,
longing to exchange defeat for victory?
Hungry,
needing to hear of a meal that satisfies?
Poor,
lacking the only things that matter?
Prisoners,
waiting to hear the order for their release?

What if all around the world
there are women and men
longing to hear of a state
where there is neither
Jew nor Arab.
black nor white,
male nor female,
establishment nor revolution?

How do you see it
as you try to read your paper
standing wedged beside me in the crowded train,
thrust into unwilling neighbourliness?

God's Rescue Operation

We are so near, you and I
and so far apart;
do you want to hear the voice of the prophet
reinterpreting your own life to you;
telling of God's rescue operation
already under way?
Do you know your need?
Do I?

> Lord Jesus,
> we pray that you
> will break into our lives,
> even though there is a part of us
> that fears your coming;
> that fears that you will
> turn our living
> inside out.
> and upside down.
>
> Teach us the true measure of our need
> that we may pray
> and look
> for that coming
> with wholehearted
> and joyful anticipation,
> eager hope,
> and a readiness to be changed.

He Has Sent Me

3rd before Christmas (Advent 2)

The spirit of the Lord is upon me because he has anointed me
Luke 4.18 REB
(But see also verses 14 – 30)

He read from the scroll of the prophet Isaiah
there, in the synagogue at Nazareth,
words which had been heard
and not heard,
for six-hundred years.
And once again as he read the familiar passage
they heard
and did not hear.

He has sent me to announce good news to the poor,
to proclaim release for prisoners
and recovery of sight for the blind.

They were poor, clinging to their poverty;
prisoners, seeking no release;
blind, lacking the desire to see.

There is an illusion of comfort and of peace
in standing outside the battle;
to be liberated,
to follow his way
could be dangerous;
the synagogue might rise against them,
they might find themselves
being hurried to a stoning
or a cross.

To let the broken victims go free,
to proclaim the year of the Lord's favour.

For those waiting with closed minds
this was too little,
altogether too little.
He had rolled up the scroll
without finishing the passage;
as though the Lord's favour
were for any
and everybody
without thought of race, or creed,
or past record.

He Has Sent Me

'Today', he said, 'in your hearing this text has come true'.

For those who waited without expectancy
this was too much,
altogether too much.
God would break into life
in some distant future,
of course he would;
but not now!
Not in the middle of morning worship!
There was no place in the liturgy for that!

*They leapt up, drove him out of the town, and took him to the brow of the hill
on which it was built, meaning to hurl him over the edge. But he walked straight
through the whole crowd, and went away.*

**From all dangerous illusions,
from the bondage of closed minds
and from life without expectancy,
Lord, in your mercy, save us.**

The Holy Scriptures

3rd before Christmas (Advent 2)

The scriptures written long ago were all written for our instruction, in order that through the encouragement they give us we may maintain our hope with perseverance.

Romans 15.4 REB

We thank you
our God and Father
for the precious gift
of the Holy Scriptures.

We thank you
for the care and the devotion
by which they have been preserved
and handed on
from generation to generation.

We thank you
for the scholarly research
and meticulous translation
by which we are provided
with texts we may trust
in our own language.

We pray
that as we read the Scriptures
for ourselves
we may be alert
to the promptings of the Spirit,
and beyond the words
on the page open before us,
may hear the Living Word
speaking to our hearts and minds,
and
hearing
may respond.

Strange Comfort

2nd before Christmas (Advent 3)

Clear a road through the wilderness for the Lord, prepare a highway across the desert for our God.

Isaiah 40.3 REB

Is there something wrong with our prayers, Lord?

We pray for the coming of the kingdom,
  and you tell us to get in training
  that we may meet the kingdom's demands.

  We pray for the coming of a new age,
  and you tell us that we need to be radically changed
  that we may become part of a new humanity.

We pray that the earth may become truly fruitful,
  and you tell us to pick up our spades
  and to start digging.

We pray that your good tidings may ring across the world,
  and you tell us to get busy
  and start by telling our neighbour.

We pray to be rescued from the desert
  and you tell us to go out into the desert
  and build a road.

We pray to be saved from all that is sordid and mean
  and you tell us to go out and seek you
  in the outcast and the despised.

We pray for peace,
  and you tell us to prepare for battle.
We pray for a bridge,
  and you tell us to learn engineering.
We pray for security,
  and you tell us to put our lives at risk.

  **Lord, we thank you
  for this strange comfort,
  which shakes our complacency,
  destroys our hope of ease,
  makes all uncertain
  and points us again
  to the pilgrim way.**

Come, Lord Jesus

Look forward to the coming of the Day of God, and work to hasten it on.
2 Peter 3.12 REB

We confess, Lord,
that we are not the people
we like others to think we are;
we even suspect
that we are not the people
we imagine ourselves to be;
but we hold on to the promise
that though you know
all the murky corners of our lives,
know us better
than we know ourselves,
you still reach out to us in love.

We also confess
that we contribute
to the injustice of this world.
Forgive us that too often
we are indifferent to the needs of others.
Forgive us our reliance
on weapons of terror.
Forgive us our discrimination
against peoples of other cultures
and our preoccupation
with our own material wellbeing.
Forgive us
that we are so unsure
of the Good News
and so hesitant
in proclaiming it.

Come, Lord Jesus,
come and make us real.
Free us from the grip of evil.
Make us new in mind and spirit.
Fill us with the energy
and the joy
of forgiven people,
for you alone are our hope,
you alone can save us.

Judgement

With justice he will judge the poor and defend the humble in the land with equity.

Isaiah 11.4 REB

So no place is left for any human pride in the presence of God. By God's act you are in Christ Jesus . . . in him we have our liberation.

1 Corinthians 1.29 – 30 REB

He stood before the court in nondescript clothes,
no papers, no fixed address.
The judge cleared his throat,
'Have you anything to say
before I pass sentence?'
What might have been his answer
had the prisoner the gift of speech
and the court the gift of hearing?

'I am condemned because your law
allows no place for me.
My crimes I freely admit:-
I am homeless, seeking shelter
where I may rear my family in modest decency.
I am stateless, seeking country
where I may belong by right in God's good earth.
I am destitute, claiming a share of the wealth
that is our common heritage.
I am a sinner, needing aid from fellow sinners.'

'You will dispose of me according to your law,
but you will not so easily dispose of him
who owns me citizen in his kingdom.
He frowns on crimes your law condones;
pride, selfishness and greed,
self-righteousness,
the worship of all things material
and the refusal to acknowledge me a brother.'

'By your law I stand condemned;
but one day you must answer
to the master of us all
for the havoc caused by your law
in his realm.'

Teach Us To Love

**1st
before
Christmas
(Advent 4)**

He has filled the hungry with good things, and sent the rich away empty.
Luke 1.53 REB

What can we say, Lord?
Your love reveals the poverty
of our loving,
Your righteousness
the inadequacy of our justice.

Forgive us our hardheartedness.
Forgive us that we are so bound-up in ourselves.
Forgive us that we are so eager to defend our rights
and so indifferent to the rights of others.
Forgive us that we can be influenced
by pressure groups
and remain indifferent to the greater needs
of those who are weak and inarticulate.

Forgive, cleanse and renew us.
Implant and nourish
your love of justice in our hearts.
Make us passionate in the cause
of those who cannot speak for themselves.
Give us the will to be advocates
for the most needy of your people.

You come as judge and as redeemer.
So deal with us that we may be fit
to share in your work of redemption
for Christ's sake.

The Word

Christmas

In the beginning the Word already was.

John 1.1 REB

I may leave the Bible
neatly shelved and dusted,
neither of us
disturbing the other;
but not the Word.

Before all,
in all,
through all,
the inescapable and eternal Word
speaks to my restlessness,
my inner discontent;
speaks to the chaos which is my life.

Rebuffed a thousand times
the Word will still be heard.
The Word unchanging
and so ever creating.
The Word unchanging
and so ever renewing.
The Word,
my adversary
and my hope.

From *News Extra*

The Word Became Flesh

Christmas *So the Word became flesh.*

John 1.14 REB

We must not be misled
by the sheer poetic beauty
of the Christmas story.
    Vision of angels;
    guiding star;
    words of ancient prophets;
    dreams of longing hearts.
Each have their place,
each signify;
but they are
not
The Word.

In stark simplicity;
in undemanding poverty;
vulnerable,
dependent,
defenceless;
a child was born.

And Mary,
Joseph,
shepherds
and wise men
gave,
    as women
    and men
    must ever give
    in love and compassion
    to a helpless infant;
and in giving
they shared
in the divine mystery;
in the purposes of God
for his creation,
and played their part
in enabling
The Word
to become
flesh.

No Room At The Inn

Christmas

There was no room for them at the inn.

Luke 2.7 REB

Beggarman, beggarman,
Born in a stable,
What do you seek of us,
What can we give?
Tiny and helpless
You ask us for blessings,
Oh, beggarman, bless us
And teach us to live.

Beggarman, beggarman
Living amongst us,
What do you seek of us
What can we give?
Hungry and homeless
You ask us for blessings,
Oh, beggarman bless us
And teach us to live.

Beggarman, beggarman,
Outcast amongst us,
What do you seek of us
What can we give?
Dispossessed, alien,
You ask us for blessings,
Oh, beggarman bless us
And teach us to live.

Beggarman, beggarman,
Dying beside us,
What do you seek of us
What can we give?
Weak and defenceless
You ask us for blessings,
Oh, beggarman bless us,
And teach us to live.

From *George*

The Significance Of Simple Things

Christmas

This will be the sign for you: you will find a baby . . .

Luke 2.12 REB

We thank you, Lord,
for all the ways in which you meet us
in our daily lives
and especially
at this time of festival,
for the significance of simple things.
For the relaxing of reserve.
For extra kindnesses
from friends and strangers.
For family reunions.
For greetings from near and far.
In all these
and in many other ways
we are reminded that you meet us lovingly
and call us to love one another in return.

We pray that we may be
so aware of
and so filled with your love,
that our response may not be confined
to these few days
but that we may make
each and every day
of the year
a celebration of your birth.

Old Man And Infant

Next before Epiphany

I have seen with my own eyes the deliverance you have made ready.
From Simeon's song. Luke 2.30 REB

Lord, as I face
the passing of the years
help me to such a faith as Simeon's.

To reach old age
and still, each day,
to wait in hope and expectation
on the Living God.

To hold an infant in my arms
and see
in that helpless burden
God's sign of rescue
yet to be accomplished.

To know the way of sorrows
and, even in that way,
praise God
for all the joys life brings.

To have so little,
and yet to still rejoice
and marvel that the Lord
has given so much.

Lord, as I face
the passing of the years
help me to such a faith as Simeon's;
for then,
whatever lies ahead of me,
the life which you have given
will be rich indeed.

Mother And Son

Next before Epiphany

Your father and I have been anxiously searching for you.
(Mary to Jesus) Luke 2.48 REB

Do we not share the anxiety
in his mother's words?
Should they have understood?
Should we,
when we discover
that our children
no longer live
as we would wish?

'Your father and I have been anxiously searching for you.'
These words were spoken
by the mother of our Lord,
so there's nothing new
about the generation gap,
that gulf which even love
finds hard to bridge.

There is pain
as well as joy
when sons and daughters grow,
strike out to find themselves,
and make their own response to life.

But so it has ever been
So it was with Joseph and Mary,
and -
God was there.

> Almighty God,
> you know what it is
> to be both child and man.
> We pray for the children we love
> as they grow towards adulthood.
> We know they will not always
> want to follow us;
> but when they do
> strike out on their own paths
> as they must;
> we pray that those paths,
> by whatever route,
> may lead them eventually
> to the Father's house.

I Would Be Wise

Epiphany

Wise men from the East came to Jerusalem, saying, 'Where is he who has been born king . . . for we have seen his star . . . and have come to worship him.'
Matthew 2.1 – 2 RSV

Source of our deepest longings,
I would be wise
with the wisdom of those
who knew that life had more to offer
than they had so far found;
in whom the spirit's quest
became a driving force,
urging them
relentlessly on and on,
until at last
they reached their journey's goal.

Source of our knowledge,
I would be wise
with the wisdom
that sought answers,
not for a fleeting moment,
but for the whole of time;
that sought eternal meaning
deep in the heart
of daily living.

Source of all truth,
I would be wise
with the wisdom
that was ready to follow
the one clue it was given;
ready to be led
from the half understood
to the deepest truths of all.

> **Lord, where do I start my quest?**
> **What clue is there for me**
> **in the world I know?**
> **What for me**
> **is the equivalent**
> **of the star**
> **which guided them?**

Abba Father

Epiphany *God has sent into our hearts the Spirit of his Son, crying, 'Abba Father!'*
Galatians 4.6 REB

Origin and life of the Universe,
we dare to call you
Father,
for we believe
that you care deeply
for each
and
every
one of us.

Yet we sense
that we cannot truly
call you Father
unless we recognise
that you are also
the Father
of every man and woman;
that we are
all your children
and so all
brothers and sisters
one of another.

Forgive us
our sins against the family
into which you have called us;
forgive us the times
when we have despised,
meanly used,
or been unjust
to other of your children.
Set us free
from the prisons we build
to separate us
from other human beings
and lead us into the freedom
which you
have created us to enjoy.

The Buck Stops Here

1st after Epiphany	*Then Jesus arrived at the Jordan from Galilee, and came to John to be baptised by him.* *Matthew 3.13 REB*

Adam blamed Eve,
Eve blamed the Serpent,
Cain took it out on Abel;
and so it has gone
on
and on
and on.

They say that Harry Truman,
when President of the United States,
placed on his desk the words
'The buck stops here'.
Good for Harry Truman!
But Lord,
that is just what you were saying,
when you went to John,
accepted the baptism of repentance
in the river Jordan,
and so identified yourself
with the whole of sinful humanity.

Since you contracted-in,
we may not contract-out.

Help us to face the fact
that we are sinners,
sharing the corporate guilt
of a rebellious world.

Bring us to repentance,
that repenting,
we may go on to
share your work
of putting wrongs to right.

Let us be among those who,
for your sake
and by your Grace,
say,
'The buck stops here'.

The Baptism of Repentance

1st after Epiphany

'There is the Lamb of God,' he said, 'who takes away the sin of the world.'
John 1.29 REB

Lord Jesus,
you went to John,
sought the baptism of repentance,
and made yourself one with us.
You voluntarily took up
the awful burden
of the sin which separates us
from the source of life,
and in this way
you broke its power
to stifle and destroy us.

But we still have to accept
what you have
done for us;
we still have to acknowledge
that we need
to be rescued.

Break down the barriers
formed by our pride
and our prejudices.
Help us to face up
to the self-centredness
of so much of our living,
and to the unworthiness
of so many of our dreams.

Saviour, Lord,
so work within us
that we may have
that change of heart
which makes it possible
for us to become a part
of your rescued community.
That, secure in your love,
we may go on to become
a part of your work
for the salvation of the world.

No Easy Calling

2nd after Epiphany

'Come, follow me, and I will make you fishers of men'
Mark 1.17 REB

Calling the Twelve together he gave them power and authority to overcome all demons and to cure diseases, and sent them out to proclaim the kingdom of God and to heal the sick.
Luke 9.1 – 2 REB

It was no easy calling:
they were to contend with the demons
that tear human beings apart,
proclaim the reign of God
to a people under the spell of usurpers,
and heal the wounds that men and women
inflict upon one another
and upon themselves.
They were to be front-line troops
in a war from which,
in this life,
there is no honourable discharge.

After this the Lord appointed a further seventy-two . . . He said to them, 'The crop is heavy, but the labourers are few'.
Luke 10.1 – 2 REB

The labourers have always been few
so I have been privileged,
for your love, Lord, has been shown to me
in the lives of parents and friends
and in the experience of a Christian fellowship.
I dare not think what heartaches
I once caused those who laboured and prayed
that I might glimpse the glory of your kingdom.
That I stand even where I do
is not of my doing
but of their patience
and your Grace.

Now I also am called to labour.
Save me from blind eyes, deaf ears
and poverty of spirit.
Help me to take my proper place and serve . . .
Yet, even as I pray, Lord,
I know that I can do nothing
in my own strength.
What is that you say?

'I will be with you always, to the end of time.'
Matthew 28.20 REB

The Voice Of The Lord

2nd after Epiphany

Speak, your servant is listening.

1 Samuel 3.10 REB

It isn't easy to recognise
that you may be present
when we are strangely restless,
seeking we know not what.

It isn't easy to recognise
that you may be speaking
when we are confronted
with a disconcerting challenge.

It isn't easy at any time
to recognise that you may be
calling us.

Yet when we do stop to listen;
when we do acknowledge
that what disturbs us
may be you seeking us;
that is still only the beginning.
To move on from hearing
to doing . . .
that is another thing altogether.

> **It was a hard task
> you gave to the boy Samuel,
> and a hard way to which you
> called him in manhood.
> Save us from imagining
> that our way should be easier.
> Save us from the illusion
> that hearing your call
> is like receiving
> an invitation to a picnic.
> And when the time comes
> that there is
> a word for us to hear,
> a work for us to do;
> give us the will to say,
> as Samuel did so long ago,
> 'Speak, your servant is listening'.**

Strange Miracle

3rd after Epiphany

So Jesus performed at Cana-in-Galilee the first of the signs which revealed his glory and led his disciples to believe in him.

John 2.11 REB

There was a wedding
at Cana-in-Galilee . . .
and Jesus and his disciples
were guests.

Strange that Jesus
should have had time to spare
for a village wedding feast;
stranger still
that he should have bothered
when the wine gave out.

'I am the bread of life,'
is a glorious affirmation
which comes ringing down the ages;
but there is something
almost frivolous
in topping up the wine
at a neighbour's wedding.

Yet this for John
was the first of the signs
by which the glory of Christ
was made known
to the world.

No pomp,
no protocol,
no carefully primed TV cameras,
not even buskers to shout,
'Walk up, walk up,
and see before your very eyes
the truly amazing miracle
of turning water into wine.'

No,
just a domestic near-disaster
touched by his presence
and transformed.
Strange,
strange and very wonderful.

The Surprising Kingdom

3rd after Epiphany

Then be sure the kingdom of God has already come upon you.
Luke 11.20 REB

Kingdom coming,
Kingdom present,
Kingdom hidden,
Kingdom seen,
Break upon myopic vision,
Let our sight be fresh and clean.

Jesus dying,
Jesus living,
Jesus servant,
Jesus king,
From our self-made prisons free us,
Joyfully our lives to bring.

Gospel joyful,
Gospel fearful,
Gospel ancient,
Gospel new,
Speak direct to our condition,
Pierce our living through and through.

Our Love And Our Perplexity

4th after Epiphany *Our forefathers had the Tent of the Testimony in the desert . . . it was Solomon who built him a house. However the Most High does not live in houses made by men.*

part of Acts 7.44, 47 – 48 REB

In the temple the blind and the crippled came to him, and he healed them.
Matthew 21.14 REB

Lord, we bring you our love,
but we also bring you our perplexity.
We are not content with the church as it is;
we are not content that we make
so little impression on the world;
we know that we are not as we should be,
but what must be changed?

Are you calling us to withdraw
from a world that is weakening us?
Or beckoning us into an ever deeper involvement
in the life of those beyond the church?
What is the difference between building bridges
and compromising the Gospel?

As the old signposts are swept away,
help us, Lord;
as we stand uncertain and hesitant,
help us, Lord;
as we hear voices bidding us both forward and back,
help us, Lord.

Searcher of minds and hearts,
teach us to distinguish between
the things to which we should hold fast
at all costs
and the things which we should gladly surrender
for your sake and the sake of the Gospel.
Help us to know you better
that we may love you better
and loving you better,
may we fear nothing
except the loss of your presence with us in the way.

The Freedom Of The Children Of God

4th after Epiphany

'I am free to do anything,' you say. 'Yes, but not everything does good . . .
Do you not know that your body is a temple of the indwelling Holy Spirit . . .?'
1 Corinthians 6.12, 19 REB

Young, healthy, educated, ambitious,
eager for every new experience;
they cried,
> 'We will be free!
> Free from restraint,
> free from tradition and petty rules,
> free to go or stay,
> free to experiment,
> free to be!
> Unhampered by the past, liberated,
> we will live as the fancy takes us.'

There came
an echo on the wind,
> 'We would be free,
> free from poverty, free from pain,
> free from oppression,
> free to eat, to work, to make a home.
> Can you not hear us, you who have so much
> yet are enslaved to your own whims;
> can you not help us, we who are
> victims of the selfish greed of others?'

As they listened a voice spoke within their hearts,
a voice older than the earth,
more youthful than the youngest of them,
> 'If you would be liberated
> from your own sense of guilt,
> surrender the freedom that is no freedom,
> accept that you are fashioned for community,
> accept the responsibilities of your humanity
> and discover the freedom
> of the sons and daughters of God'.

Lord, teach us what it means
to find, in your service,
perfect freedom.

Look For The Light

5th after Epiphany

I have come into the world as light.

John 12.46 REB

It was unobtrusive,
The Coming;
seen and not seen;
hidden by lack of concealment;
distinguished by its ordinariness.

Our fancy dresses it
with heavenly music,
light
and tinselled angels,
but that was not the way of it
at the Coming.

This is the miracle:
Not vision, star or angel;
but that it could have been
just any child,
in any land,
at any time.

Of royal blood?
Yes,
of the line of Adam;
thus no baby anywhere,
but may have it's star;
no hills so lonely
but an angel's whisper may be heard.

This is the miracle
that, looking into the eyes
of any child,
woman,
or man,
I may look straight into
the eyes of God;
may stumble on his coming
unaware.

Look For The Light

The Eternal God,
whose nature does not change
revealed himself
in time,
in a human life
and so will ever do;
and,
as at the first Christmas,
will come with human needs
that I may offer love,
and loving,
find entry to his Kingdom.

The Epilogue to *The Coming*

The Hope In Christ
(An Intercession)

5th After Epiphany

For I determined not to know any thing among you, save Jesus Christ, and him crucified.

1 Corinthians 2.2 AV

Here we are, Lord, quietly bowed in prayer,
yet something inside tells us
we should really be jumping for joy
because you come as Rescuer, as Saviour;
cleaning up the mess we make of our lives;
putting together what we pull apart.

We pray for the church.
You have called us to have a part in it's life
and despite all our failures
you have not cast us off.
We know that much of the church's witness
looks silly, weak and insignificant
to the world at large;
but you still cause its foolishness
to shame worldly wisdom,
its weakness to shame worldly strength
and its insignificance to stand as witness
against the abuse of might and power.

We pray for those who cry desperately for salvation:
- For tyranny to be overthrown.
- For the despised to be given dignity.
- For the poor to receive a proper share of the earth's resources.

We pray for our families.
Your coming on earth brought both joy
and pain to your earthly family.
Help us to know you both in the joys
and the sorrows of family life.

We remember those who have died
and pray for those who are near to death.
We are glad through sorrow and loss
for the promise that there shall be an end to death,
to mourning and crying and pain;
that the old order has passed away.

The Hope In Christ
(An Intercession)

Lord, you are the source of hope
and the inspiration of action;
so help us that,
aware of your presence,
renewed by your strength,
and anchored in your faithfulness,
we may serve you with joy
all the days of our life.

The God Given Sabbath

The Sabbath was made for man, not man for the Sabbath.
Mark 2.27 REB

Creator God,
you have made us in such a way
that our lives suffer
if we neglect the essential rhythms
of work and relaxation,
activity and rest.
We need to develop and use
the potential powers of mind and body
which you have given to us,
else our growth is stunted:
but we also need to cultivate
times of rest and refreshment
if we are to live as fully
as you intend us to live.

Long ago you gave to the people of Israel
the gift of the Sabbath.
Six days for labour;
six days to cope with the world's many demands;
but the seventh was to be a day for renewal,
a break from the pressures of daily life;
a time for souls to catch up with bodies.

For us the day of the Lord's resurrection,
a day of celebration,
is also our Sabbath,
but many fail to recognise its value.
We live in a society that has lost its way;
and we feel that the essential
rhythms of life are threatened.

Help us to recapture
the sense of the Sabbath
as a priceless gift,
as a time of joy and re-creation;
and teach us how to use your gift
in ways appropriate
to the lives we live
in the world of today.

Beyond All Dreams Of Avarice

6th after Epiphany

For everything belongs to you - Paul, Apollos and Cephas, the world, life, and death, the present and the future, all are yours - and you belong to Christ, and Christ to God.

1 Corinthians 3.21b – 23 REB

To walk among lonely hills
or along an unfrequented shore;
to watch the sunset
or the sunrise.
To revel in the
ever changing seasons
and the successive surprises
that nature springs.

To visit a busy shopping centre,
move through a lunchtime street market;
visit an art gallery
or a museum with its treasures.
To be able to enjoy
music, drama,
and to have the whole world
of literature on call.

To know through Christ
that a divided Christendom
is nonsense
and that all the riches
of the whole church
are mine to make my own.

To have other human beings
to share life's rich experiences;
to love —
and to be loved.

Am I not rich,
rich beyond all dreams of avarice?

No Easy Lessons

**9th
before
Easter**

*When his disciples had gathered round him he began to address them. And
this is the teaching he gave . . .*

Matthew 5.1 – 2 REB
(but see also the Beatitudes through to verse 12.)

We constantly discover new needs.
Magazines,
newspapers,
television,
all tell us
where we are missing out.
Yet you tell us
these things can be forgotten;
that nothing in the world
is more important
than that we should know
our need of God.

Sorrow spells loss;
the death of hopes,
the death of one we loved;
and yet you say,
'Blessed are the sorrowful'
and you gather all our sorrows
to yourself
and make them your own.

You say that the gentle
shall have the earth
for their possession;
The earth!
where the swift win the race
and the strong the battle.
Yet you were gentle,
and, owning nothing,
were completely at home
in this world.

We hear,
'Blessed are those
who hunger and thirst
to see right prevail;
they shall be satisfied'.
How can this be?

No Easy Lessons

Surely we shall never
live to see
right prevail.
You yourself
were rejected and crucified.
And yet -
YOU LIVE !

These sayings are
difficult to understand;
and there are others
which we do understand
but find hard to put into practice.

We know we should be
ready to show mercy,
have pure hearts,
be peacemakers,
be prepared to face persecution.
We know these things,
but, Lord,
you know us.

We know we'll never make it,
yet somehow,
you encourage us to keep trying.
Maybe, the more we try
the clearer it becomes;
but it can only be with your help,
These are no easy lessons.

Ears to Hear

9th before Easter

If you have ears to hear, then hear.

Luke 8.8 REB

Jesus,
Teacher and Saviour,
give us we pray, ears to hear
and minds to grasp
the things which you say to us.
Save us from the faithlessness
that writes off
your way as impossible.
Save us from the fears
that so easily
inhibit any inclination
to put your way to the test.
Save us from the blindness
which fails to distinguish
between good and evil
and from the sloth
which allows evil to pass for good.
Save us from all forms of self deception
and from the self-concern
that is unmindful of the needs of others.

When we fail, may your mercy
forgive,
restore
and renew us.
May it guide us into the way
that leads to true happiness
and bring us to the serenity
which comes from living
close to you.

The Paralysed Man

8th before Easter

I say to you, stand up, take your bed, and go home.

Mark 2.11 REB

Doctors! Faith healers! Miracle workers!
I'd tried them all, but my friends insisted
and I wasn't in any position to stop them.
That day everybody wanted him.
So, finding no other way to get near
they opened up the roof
and lowered me at his feet.

He said, 'My son, your sins are forgiven.'
But more than any words
I felt his love, his caring concern,
his whole self reaching out to me.
The past dropped away,
those futile, wasted years,
and from that moment I knew that I must live.

Whatever prison had confined my soul
the door stood open and I was free.
Free to feel, to care, to love,
and, after all those years
I stood, I walked!
But the healing would still have been a healing
though I'd never stirred a step.

All too often, Lord,
we find it difficult to believe
that your loving care can and does reach out
to our own particular dis-ease.
Yet you know our needs
better than we know them ourselves.
Teach us to listen
for the word that can make us whole
and when we hear it,
strengthen our will to respond
with all our being.

The Leper

8th before Easter

'If only you will . . . you can make me clean.'
'I will; be clean.'

Luke 5.12 REB

A leper has no friends,
for who'd come near
unless they too
had the wasting, rotting disease?
But even a leper
may hear what is happening
in the world that has disowned him.

So when I heard of the man from Nazareth
I waited.
I don't know what I hoped,
but I waited
and kept on waiting
until at last I saw him on the road.
Going as near to him as I dared
I shouted out for help.

He heard,
he not only heard
he turned and came towards me.
I knew he saw my loathsome body
as though I were stripped bare,
yet he never flinched.
His eyes, unbelievably warm and friendly,
never left me
and he came, reached out
and grasped me
as a man might clasp his dearest friend.

HE PUT HIS HANDS ON ME!
'Be whole', he said, 'Be whole!'.
HE PUT HIS HANDS ON ME!
He treated me as a human being,
and I was whole.

> **Teach us, our Saviour, by your example**
> **how to care for the unlovely**
> **and the unlovable.**
> **Strengthen our desire to be part of your body**
> **that we may be willing to face the cost**
> **of truly being your disciples,**
> **of allowing your love**
> **to become part of our living.**

They Ate And Were Satisfied

7th before Easter

'Where are we to buy bread to feed these people?'
'There is a boy here who has five barley loaves and two fish.'
John 6.5 – 9 REB

We easily forget,
but, long long afterwards
those who were there
recalled how once,
sitting in groups
on the green grass,
divisions momentarily forgotten,
he broke bread
and passed it among them
and they ate
and were satisfied.

What miracle was this,
the multiplying of loaves and fish?
Did he that day, do,
what in the wilderness
he had refused to do ?

Or was it something other,
a miracle within the heart;
self interest,
self assertion,
all put by -
 as though the kingdom
 had already come -
that as he took
the freely proffered gift
of one small boy
and blessed and break and gave,
so he released the flood of love
for too long pent within,
that each shared freely with his neighbour
and rejoiced ?

I cannot know.
But this is sure enough;
if he could take
five loaves and two small fish,
gift of a child,

They Ate And Were Satisfied

and feed a multitude;
what miracles might he work
if I as freely gave
for him to break and bless
and share today!

Save us, Lord,
from thinking of miracles
as being exclusively your concern.
Save us
from praying for miracles
without any awareness
that you might need us
to become a part of one.

You fed a multitude,
but to do it
you first required a boy
willing to give
all that he had at that moment.
It looked a futile gesture,
so little amongst so many;
but he gave it,
and you took it
and blessed it,
and the whole multitude was fed.

Lord, release in us
his simple willingness
to offer all that he had got.
Give us the will
and the faith
to be part of one
of your miracles
in the world today.

Only Comprehended By Love

7th before Easter

I have made myself everyone's servant, to win over as many as possible.
1 Corinthians 9.19 REB

Lord, Saviour;
we thank you
that when we are part of your family
we belong to a community
which cannot be tabulated by a computer
or analysed by a data processor,
but only comprehended by love.

We thank you
that we have sisters and brothers
in a relationship
stretching across the ages
and around the world,
a relationship which overrides
all barriers of race,
language
or colour.
We ask your help
to make us worthy of such a company.

Servant Lord,
you know how easily
our feelings of insecurity
can lead to self-assertion;
save us from all posturing,
all vanity and false pride,
make us so secure in the knowledge
that we are indeed held in your love
that we may joyfully follow
your ways of service
all our days.

Angel Or Tempter?

6th before Easter

Jesus was then led by the Spirit into the wilderness, to be tempted by the devil.
Matthew 4.1 REB

If only the devil would appear with cloven hoofs, horns and a tail saying, 'Good afternoon, I'm the devil, let me put a few propositions to you', life might be a little simpler. The really dangerous temptations are not those to which we fall, knowing that we do wrong; but those which appear to offer attractive, updated ways of serving the kingdom.

Angel or tempter?
Vision or mirage?
Word of God or devil's falsehood?

> 'Turn stones to bread,
> make ten blades grow in place of one,
> strike oil,
> produce an economic miracle!'

Men, women, little children
die for lack of bread,
yet others eat their fill and hunger still.
While all need bread,
no human soul can live by bread alone.

> 'Shake people from their apathy,
> stir them with wonders,
> hit the headlines!'

Yet God hires no stuntmen,
He allocates no funds for 'promotion',
His only sign, the sign of Jonah,
whose hearers turned from wickedness to live.

> 'Grasp God's world for Him!
> Drive! Compel!
> Or wait a hundred lifetimes
> and still not see the Kingdom!'

So crusades and holy wars,
so hell-fire evangelism.
But only by losing
is the Kingdom won;
and only by dying
are we brought to life.

Facing Temptation
(An Intercession)

**6th
before
Easter**

Because he himself has passed through the test of suffering, he is able to help those who are in the midst of their test.

Hebrews 2.18 REB

Help us, Lord,
for you have faced temptation,
you know how difficult it can be
to distinguish between vision and mirage,
between truth and falsehood;
help us now as we pray.

Help us in the church,
help us
– When we confuse the absence of conflict with the peace of God.
– When we equate the shaping and maintaining of committees
   and councils with serving you in the world.
– When we behave as though your presence in life were a
   past event rather than a contemporary encounter.

**Lord, help us when we are tempted.
And save us when we fall.**

Help us in the world,
help us
– When we use meaningless chatter to avoid real dialogue.
– When we allow the image presented by the media to blind
   us to the substance which lies behind it.
– When we confuse privilege with responsibility and claim
   rights when we should be acknowledging duties.
– When we allow high sounding reasons to cover unworthy
   actions.

**Lord, help us when we are tempted.
And save us when we fall.**

We pray for our families and friends and hold them before you in our thoughts . . . We especially pray for any who may be under particular pressure at this time . . .
Lord Jesus, you have passed through the test of suffering and are able to help those who are meeting that test now. We pray for all who suffer . . . We especially pray for those who suffer through their own folly, or through the folly or malice of other men and women . . .
Before the throne of God where we may find mercy and timely help we remember those who have departed this earthly life . . .
In dying, Christ broke the power of sin and death that we might enter with him into eternal life.

To Fight Or Not To Fight?

5th before Easter

He who is not with me is against me, and he who does not gather with me scatters.

Matthew 12.30 REB

Slowly he wheels
his barrow of dead leaves
across the grounds
as he has done for twenty years,
never venturing beyond the hospital gates
though they stand open.
He asks no other life,
he has become conditioned,
institutionalized.
Dare we pity him,
we from the world beyond the gates?
Are we not also conditioned,
fearful of change, do not even
the devils that haunt us
have a comforting familiarity?

'Do not call us to be heroes,
to espouse uncomfortable causes;
we are not spiritual giants.
Leave us to wheel our barrows
in the autumn sun,
even though they hold
nothing but decaying vegetation.
Why do you
call us to the conflict
we would avoid,
when all our fervent prayers
have been for peace?'

Lord, save us from so concentrating on avoiding evil
that we never do any positive good.
Renew our courage and strengthen our will
to try to do right, to intervene, contend, speak out,
when we know that is what we should be doing.
We know we shan't always *be* right,
there is too much sin in our make-up;
but when we fail
let it be as those who tried to do well,
not as those who were content to do nothing.

This Is No War Game

5th before Easter

Put on the full armour provided by God.

Ephesians 6.11 REB

Coat of mail, helmet,
shield and sword;
turn back the centuries
and, who knows,
maybe instead of jeans or formal suit
we should be dressed in armour
and, like knights of old,
be riding out on noble quests.

Or maybe not.
This is the equipment of the footsoldier,
the infantryman,
the dogsbody of all campaigns,
all countries
all ages
and all weathers.

The imagery is old.
The battle is contemporary,
urgent.
It is no war-game
to be evaluated later
over a good dinner.
It is a tough defensive action
fought by hard-pressed warriors
against half-truths,
persuasive lies,
bitter intolerance,
disguised self-interest
and every other trick the devil knows.

> You know, Lord, just how much we need
> the armour which God supplies.
> Do not let us underestimate the conflict;
> but, putting ourselves in your hands
> may we find strength to stand
> when things are at their worst,
> to stand,
> and go on standing,
> and so to complete our task.

Are We To Put All At Risk?

4th before Easter

'Anyone who wants to be a follower of mine must renounce self; day after day he must take up his cross, and follow me.'

Luke 9.23 REB

Being sensible men and women, Lord,
we try to be prudent;
we build defences about our living,
securing where we can,
and insuring as far as possible
against accidents and disasters.
We watch what we eat;
walk and drive carefully;
fit mortice locks to our doors
and make proper provision for retirement.

And in the church
we build defences against
the all-pervading secularism
of our age
and try to fashion a retreat
where we may be refreshed,
and escape for a while
the relentless pressures of the world.

Are you telling us that this is wrong?
Are we to put all at risk
and go defenceless
where men wait with hammer,
wooden cross,
and nails ?

Is this your will, Lord,
Is this really what love demands?

The Call To The Unknown

4th before Easter

'Whoever wants to save his life will lose it, but whoever loses his life for my sake will find it.'

Matthew 16.25 REB

You call us to step out
into the unknown,
and at first it sounds
exciting
and adventurous;
but when it is time for action
and we are faced with decisions,
then doubts
and forebodings arise;
we draw back;
for we cannot help thinking
of the risks involved.

It is not
that we do not want to serve you.
We earnestly pray that your Kingdom
may come alive
in the hearts of many more
men and women
who today believe
that the Church,
and the Lord of the Church,
have nothing to say to them.

For this very reason
we are reluctant
to leave known and tried ways,
lest precious experience
and cherished customs
be lost.

Help us as we hesitate.
Drive out our fearful thoughts
with visions of what may be won;
and strengthen our will
to continue on the road
to which you call us
wherever it may lead.

Truth Is Frightening

3rd before Easter	*In their presence he was transfigured - the disciples fell on their faces in terror.* *Matthew 17.2,6 REB*

The moment of vision can be shattering. All of a sudden we are brought up against the otherness of God. So it was with Moses before the burning bush, Isaiah in the Temple, Saul on the way to Damascus. Going apart with Jesus the disciples may at first have felt a little pride and self satisfaction; they were his close friends and confidants. Then suddenly, there is a great gulf, they find themselves far from him, speechless, or muttering nonsensical nothings.

We come to you, the human Christ,
teacher, healer, leader,
lover of children,
companion of our way.
We have committed ourselves
to the service
of the God you have revealed;
we support the church and it's witness.
We know that we are sinners,
but we also know
that you will meet our follies
with an all-forgiving love.

Then we realise
that this truth is only a half-truth.
We have no right to expect
an all too easy forgiveness.
You are God as well as man
and our sins make a gulf
which may only be bridged
at terrible cost.

Truth is frightening!
Truth about the holiness of God
and human sin.
When the scales fall from our eyes
and we begin to know ourselves
for what we are
we are horrified by what we see.
Yet however awful the awakening
we dare not ask to escape it,
for it is only by facing this truth
that we can open the way
for your work to be done in us,
for the gulf to be bridged.

68

The Serving Community

3rd before Easter

We proclaim Christ Jesus as Lord, and ourselves as your servants for Jesus sake.
2 Corinthians 4.5 REB

Whenever we begin
to take you seriously, Lord,
you turn our world upside down.
You tell us to measure life
not by what we can obtain,
but by what we are able to give.

You show
how the most precious gifts
may be given out of poverty.

The final meal
with your disciples,
which we recall with thanksgiving
every time we gather at your table,
was in a borrowed room.

Your final agony of prayer
was in a borrowed garden.

On the cross
you were utterly helpless
in the hands of your enemies
yet you reached out
in loving compassion
and rescuing power
to the whole world.

We cannot hope to match
your giving of yourself,
yet we pray
that something of your life
may live in us
that we may be servants
in your world
for your sake.

No Easy Road

2nd before Easter

If anyone is to serve me, he must follow me.

John 12.26 REB

The road Christ trod
is not listed by the AA,
or maintained by any highway authority.
At best it is a footpath,
sometimes ploughed
or blocked,
and often it is painful
to the feet.

To tread it we must learn to be;
– So great that we can accept being nothing.
– So strong that we have no desire to inflict injury.
– So loving that we can endure hatred.
– So sure of the truth by which we live
   that we can bear to be called deceivers.
– So vitally alive that we are prepared when needs be,
   to die.

Lord Jesus Christ,
the road you trod
for our sakes led to rejection,
and a cross on a rubbish tip;
but our faith is
that it was not the end of the journey.
You live
and travel with us,
as you have travelled
with countless others
across the ages.

> **Encourage us, Lord, we pray,
> when we are in danger of losing heart.
> Hold us when we stumble.
> Bring us back to the path when we stray;
> for despite all our weaknesses
> and our follies
> our hearts are set
> on following in your way.**

Triumph Through Suffering
(An Intercession)

Can you drink the cup I am to drink?

Matthew 20.22 REB

Dietrich Bonhoeffer was executed in the concentration camp at Flossenburg on 9th April 1945. In *Letters and Papers from Prison* he wrote,

> *There remains for us only the very narrow way, often extremely difficult to find, of living every day as if it were our last, and yet living in faith and responsibility as though there were to be a great future.*

Let us pray that we, with all Christ's people, may learn to live each day to the full.
Let us quietly affirm in our hearts our faith in God's great future.

All things are transitory.
But God's love lasts for ever.

> *It is only by living completely in this world that one learns to have faith . . . In so doing we throw ourselves into the arms of God, taking seriously, not our own sufferings, but those of God in the world.*

Let us ask Christ to help us to take seriously the call to live for him *in* the world.
Let us praise God for his giving of himself in Christ that the world may be saved, and acknowledge his call to us to work with him for that salvation.

All things are transitory.
But God's love lasts for ever.

Let us pray for those who suffer; especially . . .

> *In suffering, the deliverance consists in our being allowed to put the matter out of our hands into God's hands.*

Let us particularly pray for those who find it hard to believe in the love of God, that they may find him and learn to yield themselves into his hands.

All things are transitory.
But God's love lasts for ever.

Triumph Through Suffering
(An Intercession)

When he knew his execution was near Dietrich Bonhoeffer wrote,

Death is the supreme festival on the way to freedom.

Let us remember those who have died. Especially . . .

All things are transitory
But God's love lasts for ever.

May God in his mercy lead us through these times; but above all, may he lead us to himself.

The Foolishness Which Confounds Our Wisdom

1st before Easter (Palm Sunday)

'Who is this?' people asked.

Matthew 21.10 REB

Across the ages ring two cries
conflicting,
yet woven together,
'Blessings on him who comes in the name of the Lord!'
'Crucify him!'
Linked to the end of time
by twisted human nature
both wanting
and rejecting God.
In a moment of history
Jesus enters Jerusalem
and goes to Calvary;
yet these events belong to every age,
and in every age
men shout 'Hosanna!'
and are consenting to his death.

Lord, you come as one
who has a rightful claim upon us
yet without pomp, or weapons or intrigue.
Riding a donkey
you are ready to be laughed at, scorned,
beaten, crucified.
You know what we are
and what the end must be
yet still you come.
Your foolishness confounds our wisdom
your weakness overthrows our strength,
you reach out towards us in love,
a love so easy to deny,
so hard to escape.
We fail you, we reject you,
we have no claim upon you.
Yet still you claim us,
and for your love's sake we dare to pray,
'Remember us, and save us into your Kingdom'.

Holy Week Meditation

1st before Easter (Palm Sunday)

Their judgement was unanimous: that he was guilty and should be put to death.
Mark 14.64 REB

Lord Jesus,
when you entered Jerusalem
many spread a carpet of palm branches
before you and shouted,
'Blessings on him who comes
in the name of the Lord'.
We too would join
in the joyful welcome
as you come to claim your own.

You challenged men and women
to live as citizens
of a kingdom,
not after the fashion
of the world,
but rather with a mission
to transform the world.
Help us,
as your servants,
to live fully human lives
enjoying and serving the world;
but save us
from being possessed and destroyed
by worldliness.

When you were handed over
to the authorities,
flogged,
and put to death;
men and women could still not escape
the fact that your living
testified to a different order.
You reign,
even on the cross;
always and everywhere,
you are in control.
May we learn to love your way
and desire to follow in it.

Holy Week Meditation

On that cross
you prayed forgiveness
for those who,
through spite or malice,
through cowardice or indifference,
brought about your rejection
and death.
Their sins are our sins.
In them we were present.
We too need your forgiveness,
your salvation.

When you were raised from the dead
men and women realised
in wonder
that in your living and dying
they had seen
the very love of God Himself,
and that that love
was for all peoples
and for all times.

We pray that the love
which is in you
may live in us
and flow through us,
now and forever.

The One Who Serves

Maundy Thursday

He humbled himself, and was obedient, even to the point of death, death on a cross.

Philippians 2.8 REB

I have set you an example: you are to do as I have done for you.
John 13.15 REB

Climbing the stairs
to that
Upper Room,
each was shut in his
separate,
private world
of dreams and nightmares.
They sat at table
in uncomfortable neighbourliness,
the dust of the streets still on them;
together,
yet not together;
each man imprisoned within himself.

Water and basin stood untouched,
none willing to be servant
to the others
until Jesus,
rising,
took towel,
water and basin
and washed their feet,
servant and master in one.

Even as they protested
they knew that it had always been so;
always would be so.
his body broken for them;
his life poured out
that they might live;
and with them
every soul
in every land
in every age.

The One Who Serves

Years pass,
faces change;
yet still to that Table
come disciples
soiled by the world,
divided . . .

Again the Lord comes as servant
and we know,
amid all that poisons
human relationships,
we are a part
of that broken body,
renewed by that freely given life.

Beyond all words
and symbols,
HIMSELF,
the Life,
the Truth,
the Way.

> **Lord, you truly said,**
> **'A servant is not greater than his master**
> **nor a messenger than the one who sent him.'**
> **We dare not claim**
> **that we are**
> **valiant witnesses;**
> **but give us grace**
> **as needs arise,**
> **willingly to gird ourselves**
> **with the towel**
> **and follow you in humble**
> **yet joyful service.**

At The Cross

Good Friday

We have a law; and according to that law he ought to die.

John 19.7 REB

Helpless,
he hung spreadeagled
between earth and sky;
yet still the conflict was not over,
in agonising waves of consciousness
came mocking cries,
'He saved others, but he cannot save himself.'
With monstrous doubts the enemy
bombarded the last defences
of mind and spirit.

To live for love
and stir up so much hatred!
'If only you had filled their stomachs
or, better still,
proclaimed a holy war,
you would at least have died a hero!'
Was that the enemy,
or did those words
come from another part of his own self?

Was love illusion?
Was costly, bitter, sacrificial love
a mirage with no substance in eternity?
No answer,
but the mocking of the crowd
and evil's doubts . . .
'My God, my God why hast Thou forsaken me?'

> **Saviour Christ,**
> **you have plumbed the deepest depths**
> **of human agony**
> **and taken that pain**
> **into the very heart of the Godhead.**
> **In awe and wonder we give thanks**
> **that we have a God**
> **who feels the awfulness**
> **of our darkest moments.**
> **We pray for those who at this time**
> **are plunged into the depths**
> **that they may know their agony**
> **is shared by you**
> **and that they are not abandoned.**

Mary Magdalene - Friday

Good Friday

A number of women were also present - Among them was Mary of Magdala.
Matthew 27.55 – 56 REB

Mary Magdalene speaks –

They used to say I had seven devils;
not that the young men
liked me any the less for that.
Seven devils! Maybe I had,
and one was a devil of anger
who returned to me today.
God, was I angry!
Angry with Caiaphas, Pilate, the soldiers;
angry with everyone,
but mostly, you might as well know it,
angry with you,
the crowd that sits and watches,
cheers and boos and sucks peppermints.
For you it was just another gory news item
while you waited for the big spectacular
billed for peak viewing time
later in the evening.
For him it was everything he had lived for
thrown back in his face:
and he cried on the Father to forgive,
forgive Pilate and Caiaphas, the soldiers, the crowds;
to forgive you - and me.
Yes me. To forgive my anger,
and the old trick of throwing the blame on somebody else.
I could have built a wall to shield me
from his curses, but not his forgiveness.
And so the anger's gone,
like those seven devils went when he first met me.
And I see only blindness and ignorance and folly.
Father forgive us, we do not know what we are doing.

From *One Friday in Eternity*

Mary Magdalene – Easter Morning

Easter Day

But Mary stood outside the tomb weeping.

John 20.11 REB

Mary Magdalene speaks –

O God, where shall I go, what shall I do?
No hope, no purpose,
nothing but endless empty hours.
He made me live and since that day
I have drawn strength from him.
O my Master, my Lord,
why did you have to die?
We're all so terribly adrift.
We thought we were supporting you,
but now I see we were a weight
you carried every day.

She turns to the tomb

You ask me why I weep ?
Weep! I want to batter on heaven's doors
and shriek in protest
that it should come to this:
that I cannot even say,
'What once was him is here'
and at least touch the rock for memory's sake.

She turns and sees a figure standing

Are you the keeper of this garden?
For if you are, tell me for pity's sake
where you have taken him . . .
You say my name as only . . .

Master!

Yes Lord, I'll tell them.
I'll tell the world!

From One Friday in Eternity

A Gloriously Inverted View Of Life

**1st
after
Easter**

Thinking it was the gardener, she said, 'If it is you sir, who removed him, tell me where you have laid him, and I will take him away'. Jesus said, 'Mary!' She turned to him and said, 'My Master'.

adapted from John 20.15 – 16 REB

It was impossible!
Beyond hope
or expectation;
it couldn't be,
and yet, it was!
Now she knew
what deep in her heart
she had always known:
in Him was love that nothing could destroy,
in Him the healing sought through bitter pain,
in Him the good we dream in evil days,
in Him the life that holds us beyond death.
She had a message now
for all the world:
> The Lord is risen!
> He is risen indeed!

Give to us, Lord,
the gloriously inverted view of life
which was yours,
that we may see where the true triumph
and the true glory lie.
You are winning victories in the world
in our time;
help us to recognise them
and to acclaim them for what they are.
You call us to the way of the cross,
give us grace to tread it with resurrection joy
both in our hearts and on our faces.

Pull Back The Bolts!

1st after Easter

Late that same day . . . the disciples were together behind locked doors
John 20.19a REB

'Who's there?'
Starting at every sound
they slumped behind locked doors,
defeated,
shattered;
in such an earth
there was no place for him
or for his God.

Jesus came and stood among them. 'Peace be with you!' he said.
John 20.19b REB

'Peace be with you!'
That voice -
in this room
this very room?
Not held by lock or bar,
here,
in this very room,
he lives?

'As the Father sent me, so I send you.' Then he breathed on them, saying, 'Receive
the Holy Spirit!'
John 20.21 – 22 REB

Pull back the bolts!
We must away
He was here
but now
he's out ahead of us;
out in the conflicts of the world:
the world for which he died;
the world for which he lives!

It Was The Lord!

1st after Easter

They described what had happened on their journey and told how he had made himself known to them in the breaking of the bread.

Luke 24.35 REB

A meeting during a journey.
New meaning given
to long familiar words.
A shared meal.
In such simple things you come,
dispelling gloom,
renewing hope,
restoring life.
Yet often we are blind
and only afterwards
say,
'That day it was the Lord!'

**Lord, help us to see more clearly
that we may recognise you near,
not only in the solemn churchly rite,
but in the basic stuff of life;
the road we travel,
the people we meet,
and the bread we break.**

83

This I Believe

2nd after Easter

'I have come that they may have life, and may have it in all its fullness.'
John 10.10 REB

This I believe:
that you are true,
and may be trusted
to the end of time
and then beyond,
to whatsoever is
when time's no more.

This I believe:
that you are love,
love that goes with me
through the joy, the pain,
the faith, the doubt,
and all the tangled threads
that make my days,
and holds me fast.

This I believe:
that you are life,
life that renews me
though the body age
and senses fail,
life with the vibrant power
to vanquish death.

Way for my feet,
goal for my journey's end;
my faith is marred by doubt,
my living scarred by sin;
I have no claim upon you,
yet your love is such
that you have said,
'I will be with you always':
THIS I BELIEVE!

Even New Life Has It's Problems

2nd after Easter

But that night they caught nothing. Morning came, and Jesus was standing on the beach.

John 21.3 – 4 REB

Lord,
I know that you are risen
and that you are living
in the world today.
I know that every morning
should be begun in hope,
and every Sunday made
a victory celebration;
but life still has it's problems.

How do I work out my faith
in my day to day life ?
I don't find it easy
to talk about you.
I seldom see clearly
what I am meant to do.
Much of the time
I seem to be muddling through
and there are moments
when I'm quite lost.

Lord,
I know that I cannot expect
to live continually bathed
in some warm eternal glow;
but for all the times
of unrewarded effort,
of seemingly wasted hours
and spiritual emptiness,
I ask that you
strengthen my will
to hold on,
until once again
I have
your voice to guide me,
your presence to renew.

The Life We Seek

3rd after Easter *Jesus said, 'I am the resurrection and the life. Whoever has faith in me shall live, even though he dies; and no one who lives and has faith in me shall ever die. Do you believe this?'*

John 11.25 – 26 REB

Then he raised his voice in a great cry: 'Lazarus, come out.'
John 11.43 REB

Life now!

That you come,
not merely as a future hope,
but as a new dimension
to present living;
this is what we find it hard to grasp.

You tell us that born,
we must be born again;
that living,
we must come to life.
You call us,
and we stumble
from the darkness
which we only recognise as a grave
as we begin to move out towards the light.

Dare we step out
into this blinding brilliance?
What problems,
what dangers await us,
what new demands will be made on us?

This new birth is painful;
this breaking free from shrouds
which have covered our decay
with a vestige of decency.
We hear the call:
strengthen our will to answer,

> **'Lord live in us
> and make us live,
> that we may step out
> into the light
> and share your resurrection miracle'.**

Feed My Sheep

3rd after Easter

'Feed my sheep — If it should be my will that he stay until I come, what is it to you? Follow me.'

John 21.17, 22 REB

'Feed my sheep', you said;
it sounds simple enough,
yet it's unlikely that those sheep will be found
patiently waiting in a gated pasture.

'Feed my sheep';
but they will have to be sought;
and where that search will lead,
and what the cost, who can know
until their work is done.

Will our way
be easier or harder,
more or less glorious
than that of our fellow shepherds?
We ask, but you do not answer;
instead, you tell us that given a task
our part is simply to perform it faithfully.

> **Lord, we are grateful**
> **that you have made yourself known to us**
> **as the Good Shepherd;**
> **yet we realise that just because you are**
> **the Good Shepherd**
> **you will not allow us**
> **to hide behind the illusion**
> **that as your sheep**
> **we have nothing to do but to be cared for.**
> **You call us to discover powers**
> **hidden within ourselves**
> **that we may share your work**
> **of loving and serving,**
> **just as you love and serve us.**
> **We know it won't be easy,**
> **but we ask you to prepare and encourage us**
> **that we may indeed be ready**
> **to go about your business**
> **wherever it may lead.**

The Pilgrim Way

4th after Easter	*'I am the way, the truth, and the life.'*
	John 14.6 REB

'I am the way.'
But not for unthinking travellers
who neglect map and compass
and go ill-briefed,
ill-shod,
ill-clad.
You call us to a pilgrimage,
but you do not promise
any easy path.

'I am the truth.'
But not for intellectual hair-splitting;
not to be codified or fossilized.
Declared in flesh and blood
this truth IS Christ
and woman or man
we are either
for him or against him.

'I am the life.'
Life!
Yet life
that has at its heart a death.
It is a resurrection
preceded by a cross.
Freely given
it must still be grasped
and being grasped
be lived with painful joy.

**Lord, I am a traveller
who often strays.
Strengthen my will
to walk in the way,
to live in the truth
to take hold of the life;
that holding I may be held,
now and forever.**

Nine Gifts In One

4th after Easter

Be guided by the Spirit and you will not gratify the desires of your unspiritual nature. That nature sets its desires against the Spirit . . . but the harvest of the Spirit is love, joy, peace, patience, kindness, goodness, fidelity, gentleness and self-control.

Galatians 5.16 – 23 REB

Nine gifts, yet one
one harvest
in a rich diversity.
LOVE,
which is to care
and care,
and go on caring;
and JOY
a bubbling spring
rising in the heart
and replenished
by each counted blessing.
PEACE,
the refuge of tranquillity
which,
when under pressure,
we may yet find
deep within ourselves;
and PATIENCE,
the constancy
that steadily endures
however grim the way.
KINDNESS
bestows
without creating debtors;
GOODNESS
does right
by those most needing aid.
FIDELITY,
a rock
of utter dependability,
and GENTLENESS,
the strength
which never is asserted out of place.
Lastly comes SELF-CONTROL,
the victory over passion
by which
we become consistent
through and through.

Down But Not Out

5th after Easter

'In the world you will have trouble. But courage! The victory is mine; I have conquered the world.'

John 16.33 NEB

'To the angel of the church at Smyrna write; I know how hard pressed you are and poor – and yet you are rich.'

Revelation 2.8 – 9 NEB

We have sisters and brothers under pressure
because of the Gospel;
giving out of their destitution,
faithful through persecution,
tiny minorities in a hostile society,
outnumbered, but not outlived.

Like the church in Smyrna.
Accounted insignificant, you saw their value.
Accounted poverty-stricken, you saw their riches.
Accounted weak, you saw their strength.
It is not our strength,
but our weakness that finds you near;
your signs the stable, wilderness and cross.

We too are under pressure,
different pressure;
pressure at home, at work,
pressure of age, of health,
pressures in the church,
pressures in the world.
If we were more faithful
would the pressures be less,
or greater?

> **We pray for our sisters and brothers
> under pressure because of the Gospel,
> giving out of their destitution,
> faithful through persecution,
> tiny minorities in a hostile society,
> outnumbered, but not outlived.**

> **We praise you because wherever
> the church is under pressure you are there.
> Give us grace that we also may
> stand against unworthy pressures;
> live in the world
> without being possessed by the world,
> hold to the faith,
> and be numbered among your faithful people.**

O Crucified And Risen Lord
(An Easter Hymn)

5th after Easter

A little while, and you see me no more; again a little while, and you will see me.
John 16.16 REB

O crucified and risen Lord
Destroy the bonds that bind us tight,
Release us from our greed and pride
And lead your people into light.
> Born, once, we must be born again,
> Alive, we still must learn to live.

From dawdling by an empty tomb,
From eyes that look and fail to see,
From fear of death and fear of life
Lord, set your foolish people free.
> Born, once, we must be born again,
> Alive, we still must learn to live.

From thinking heaven's far away,
From fearing change and fearing strife,
From clinging to a world that's past,
Lord, lead your people into life.
> Born, once, we must be born again,
> Alive, we still must learn to live.

O triumph found beyond defeat,
O good men dream in evil days,
O love no evil could destroy
Possess our lives and shape our ways.
> Born, once, we must be born again,
> Alive, we still must learn to live.

O crucified and risen Lord,
You are the Life, the Truth, the Way,
Let Easter dawn blaze on our souls
And make us children of the day.
> Born, once, we must be born again,
> Living, we still must learn to live.

This first appeared in *All Year Round* with the tune 'O crucified and risen Lord' and the chorus:
> Born, we must be reborn
> Living we must learn to live.

The metre for the hymn in this form is 88.88.88 and it may be sung to Sussex Carol or Melita.

The Risen Lord
(An Intercession)

**6th
after
Easter
(Ascension)**

I will be with you always, to the end of time.

Matthew 28.20 REB

Crucified and risen Lord, we pray for the church.
Save us from dawdling by an empty tomb.
Save us from bondage to the past.
Save us from the hypnotic fascination of decay and death
and make your church to know resurrection.

Living Lord Jesus, One with the Father in glory,
Save us from behaving as though that glory had taken you
far from us.
Save us from standing helplessly, waiting for something,
we know not what, to happen.
Save us from projecting your kingdom into some distant
future and enable us to recognise that kingdom at work
all about us.

> **The Lord is risen.**
> **He is risen indeed.**

Saviour Christ, we pray for the peoples of the world.
Hanging on the cross you gave hope to a rebel at your side
and prayed for those who condemned you to that violent
death.
We too live amid violence.
The violence of subversion,
of repressive government,
and all the subtle violence by which the powerful
seek to impose their will on the weak.
None of us are free from its taint.
You alone can give the victory over the violence of the
world and of our hearts.

Save us Lord. Give us the will and the power to share your
victory.

> **The Lord is risen.**
> **He is risen indeed.**

The Risen Lord
(An Intercession)

Living Lord, we pray for our society,
entombed in material possessions
and oppressed with ever changing fears.
Many know no better hope than that they may enjoy a few
years of quiet retirement before the end.
Release us from this living death.
Cause us to live with the life you alone can give.

The Lord is risen
He is risen indeed.

Lord, you know what it is to suffer pain, degradation and
rejection and to die an outcast.
We pray for all who suffer . . .
May they know you as one who shares their agony
and enables them to share your triumph.

With thanksgiving for the life that was poured out for us
and in joyous hope of the life you call us to share, we
remember those dear to us who have died . . .
As in Adam all die,
So in Christ will all be brought to life.

Now to the King of all worlds, immortal, invisible, the
only God, be honour and glory for ever and ever, Amen.
1 Timothy 1.17 NEB

Ascension

6th after Easter (Ascension)

He was lifted up before their very eyes, and a cloud took him from their sight.
Acts 1.9 REB

Lost to sight in the clouds!
Taking off,
jet propelled like a human rocket
to return to —
where?

Is that how it was,
the Ascension?

or . . .

Caught up into all the glory of God
and so here —
and everywhere;
no longer imprisoned by physical limitations
unseen,
but not
unexperienced.

One with the Father,
Jesus takes
into the Godhead
all that it means
to be human.

And so I know
that I am known,
by the Almighty;
known,
and
understood.

The Real Babel

Pentecost

That is why it is called Babel, because there the Lord made a babble of the language of the whole world.

Genesis 11.9 REB

Sprechen Sie Deutsch?
Ydych chi'n siarad Cymraeg?
Apni ki bangla janen?
Parlez vous Francais?
Pe e tautala i le gagana Samoa?
Do you speak English?

Similar questions —
Different words!
Different sounds!
Yet if the Lord confused the speech of the world
he also provided the means
by which the confusion might be overcome.
Take determination,
study,
practice,
and a dash of love,
and the Doctor of Philosophy
for whom the whole world has become a village
may sit down with a peasant
whose village is the whole world
and there will be understanding.

The great divide, the really great divide,
is between those who speak the same words
with different intent
divided by a determination to conceal
rather than to communicate;
divided by suspicion, pride or fear.
Boardroom speaks with shop floor,
government with rebel,
manufacturer with competitor;
but the words are empty husks
despite a common mother tongue.

> **Lord, teach us to put aside**
> **the language of suspicion, pride and fear,**
> **the greeting without warmth,**
> **the word that belies the heart,**
> **the half truth that is no truth;**
> **lest the tower we are so busy building**
> **in this modern Babel**
> **all, and crush us all.**

Life In The Spirit
(An Intercession)

Pentecost

After this I shall pour out my spirit on all mankind.

Joel 2.28 REB

Spirit of power,
we find it hard to truly come together in the church
even within a single congregation,
how shall we learn to be one family,
loving and serving the whole of humanity?

Lead us into such unity of purpose
that we may receive power;
not the power to threaten or destroy
but the power to restore waste places.
Use us to declare your glory
that blind eyes may see,
deaf ears hear,
and the cynical be brought to faith.

> **Spirit of the Living God
> Hear our prayer.**

Spirit of truth,
we live in a modern Babel
where words are used to conceal meaning
rather than to make it plain.
Lead the peoples of the world
into such a love of truth
that nation may speak with nation,
not seeking to confuse,
but to understand and to be understood;
so that trust is created out of which
a truly international community may be born.

> **Spirit of the Living God
> Hear our prayer.**

Creator Spirit,
you give us the capacity
to dream dreams and to see visions,
but because we exalt ourselves and our desires
to the place which is yours alone
our visions are visions of horror
and our dreams nightmares.

96

Life In The Spirit
(An Intercession)

Raise up artists and prophets among us
with the will and the ability
to inspire and cleanse our society,
to set hearts aflame
and turn our eyes to the heights.

> **Spirit of the Living God**
> **Hear our prayer.**

Source of all comfort,
we pray for the lonely,
the sick, the sad, the bereaved
and all who suffer or are ill at ease.
We claim for them the gift of your peace
that troubled hearts may be set at rest
and fears banished.

> **Spirit of the Living God**
> **Hear our prayer.**

Giver of life,
we remember those who have died . . .
May they enter into the Kingdom
where your presence is all in all.

> **Spirit of the Living God**
> **Hear our prayer.**

Too Small A Vision?

1st after Pentecost (Trinity)

Before the foundation of the world he chose us in Christ to be his people, to be without blemish in his sight, to be full of love . . . that the universe, everything in heaven and on earth, might be brought into a unity in Christ.

Ephesians 1.4, 10 REB

We confess with shame
that the very sense of being chosen
and the desire to be a church without blemish,
has led to the separation
of Christian from Christian.
We may not have denounced
or persecuted others,
but we have too easily accepted
the divided inheritance.
We have made moves
towards better understanding,
but we have not passionately desired
to bridge the gulfs.
We have not loved one another as we should.

We thank you for the way
in which you have led us, despite ourselves,
towards the breaking down of barriers
and the overcoming of deep-set fears,
suspicions and prejudices.
We thank you for the growing realization
that theological differences
and varieties of administration
can live together within your body.

Sometimes, Lord, we dare to dream of a day
when the whole Church on earth
will become one in love and one in purpose.
Then a doubt arises; is the unity of the Church
too small a vision?
Is it diverting us from directing our prayers
and our energies to a larger hope,
the unity of all humankind,
– No longer despoiling Planet Earth.
– No longer striving one against the other.
But seeking to live in harmony
with all peoples and with the whole creation?
Is this what you are calling us to work towards?
Is this what you are urging us to proclaim?

Too Large A Task?

1st after Pentecost (Trinity)

'If you knew me you would know my Father too.'

John 14.7 REB

We rejoice that you are a God
who breaks into history
bringing light to our darkness,
intervening on behalf of the needy,
raising up rescuers for the oppressed.

But your coming also reveals
the shoddiness of our service.
Men and women cry for relief
from miseries of which
we have little experience.
How can we hear the cry of the needy
as you hear it?
How can we be moved with your compassion,
feel as you do
the wrongs done to your children?

Lord, forgive us that in your church
we find it so hard to put first things first;
that we strain at gnats and swallow camels.
Do not cast us on time's rubbish heap.
Help us to see more clearly your priorities
and to put human need before careful orthodoxy.

Give us hearts to know you as we should.
Give us the will and the strength
to reflect your nature to the world,
even though much we cling to must be destroyed
that the hungry may be filled with good things.

All Things In Common

2nd after Pentecost	*They met constantly to hear the apostles teach, and to share the common life, to break bread, and to pray . . . All the believers agreed to hold everything in common . . . and, breaking bread in their homes, they shared their meals with unaffected joy.*
	Acts 2.42, 44, 46 REB

Like the summers of our youth,
it was already a memory
when Luke wrote,
telling of a people
in the dawn
of the Spirit's power,
utterly at one in all things.

Was it memory
or dream?
A dream of how it should have been,
must be,
will be
by God's grace
when his work in us
is fully done.

Memory,
or dream,
or whisper of the Spirit in the heart?
That they could hold
all things in common
and share their meals
with unaffected joy.

> **Enable us, Lord Jesus,
> to carry the reality of the Kingdom
> deep in our hearts.
> Save us from little-mindedness
> and the fears
> that would deny others
> their part in the good things
> given for all to enjoy.
> Lead us in the ways of true fellowship
> in our homes,
> in our churches
> and in the world at large.**

Also Your Children

2nd after Pentecost

Bring in the poor, the crippled, the blind, and the lame ... I want my house full.
Luke 14.21, 23 REB

Lord of the outcast
and the dispossessed,
forgive us as the number
of homeless people
increases in our land.

Forgive us that deep in our hearts
we do not want to know their problems,
do not want to acknowledge
that these women, men,
and children
are your people,
loved by you;
that they have been created
to be your sisters
and brothers
with us
in this world,
where nothing is lacking
save the will
to create true community.

Forgive us that we leave you
to make the pilgrimage
with families grudgingly placed
in bed and breakfast accommodation.

Forgive us that we leave you
to share with the evergrowing company
of those sleeping rough,
glad to find
even a cardboard box
for shelter.

Forgive us that we leave you
to the bitterness and cynicism
of young men
and young women
increasingly alienated

Also Your Children

by a society
which offers them little hope.

Forgive us when we self-righteously
deplore the violence
that erupts in our cities,
but refuse to acknowledge
that we ourselves
are part of the problem.

Forgive us and save us
from our narrow, individualistic goals.
Save us from cultivated blindness
and convenient deafness.
Save us before it is too late
and we hear the words
'Inasmuch as you did it not to these
my sisters and brothers you did it not to me.'

No Other Name

3rd after Pentecost

In all the world no other name has been granted . . . by which we can be saved.
Acts 4.12 REB

'No other name!'
Is salvation then for the few,
the favoured few;
is heaven for the lucky ones
who have learned
to recite the proper formulas;
attend the right ceremonies,
live by the prescribed rules,
and so become numbered
amongst the 'elect'.
Is that it?

Or does
'No other name!'
mean that salvation
through Jesus Christ
is salvation
through what he was,
and is —
the embodiment of the love
at the heart of God?
Love reaching out
at the cost
of a crucifixion
to restore
his fallen creation to Himself?
A love so great
that it encompasses
everyone,
everything;
so great
that it is content
with nothing less
than the salvation
of the whole creation?

Prayer In Time Of Difficulty

3rd after Pentecost

Shine like stars in a dark world.

Philippians 2.17 REB

Lord, as we face both the major difficulties
and the petty irritations of life today,
let us lose neither our sense of proportion
nor our sense of humour.
Help us to retain an inner serenity,
and when our patience is strained to breaking point,
remind us again of your infinite patience with us.
Renew our flagging spirits
with the brightness of your presence
so that no shadow may long oppress us;
and when we do feel low,
save us from spreading gloom that darkens
the light by which others are trying to live.
Help us to face each day as it comes
with courage and quiet confidence
and teach us quickly to forget our woes
but to have a long memory for our blessings.

The Inner Spring Of The Water Of Life

4th after Pentecost	*Whoever drinks the water I shall give will never again be thirsty. The water that I shall give will be a spring of water within him, welling up and bringing eternal life.* *John 4.14 REB*

We are thirsty!
We have tried to quench our thirst,
at many wells,
but the craving remains,
we are still unsatisfied.

We have refurbished our homes,
re-equipped our wardrobes,
stocked up our freezers
and invested in the latest
technological wonders.

We have
changed our car,
changed our diet,
changed our job,
changed our partner.

We have gone on the holiday
to surpass all holidays,
but we are still unsatisfied,
still thirsty.

Are you saying, Lord,
that the one thing that really matters
is still missing?
That we shall go on being thirsty
until we start again,
with you?

> **Saviour Christ,
> help us to recognise
> where the streams of living water
> are to be found,
> that no longer chasing
> after each fresh mirage
> we may come to drink
> of that inner spring which you supply,
> the spring that never runs dry.**

When The Springs Of My Life Run Dry

4th after Pentecost

Whoever drinks the water I shall give will never again be thirsty. The water that I shall give will be a spring of water within him, welling up and bringing eternal life.

John 4.14 REB

When Something goes tragically wrong in our life, maybe when we are faced with a particularly painful bereavement; we can go through a period where nothing brings relief, even our prayers seem unanswered. The following, originally put into the mouth of Mary, Mother of Jesus, standing at the foot of the cross, expresses the thought that at such a time the temptation to withdraw into ourselves must be resisted. It is as we reach out to others that we are most likely to discover the 'water of life' flowing again for our renewal.

When the springs of my life run dry
And my spirit is heavy with grief,
I must not hide in a solitary place
For my spirit must find relief.
Though I've only my grief
I must share my grief
That my spirit may find relief.

When the springs of my life run dry
And my heart is racked with pain,
I must not hide in a solitary place
For the springs must flow again.
Though I've only my pain
I must share my pain
That the springs may flow again.

When the springs of my life run dry
And my friends are far and few,
I must not hide in a solitary place
For my love must blossom anew,
Through my grief and my pain
I must love once again
That my life may blossom anew.

From *One Friday in Eternity.*

Prayer For The City

5th after Pentecost

And should not I pity Nineveh that great city . . .

Jonah 4.11 RSV

Pressing in upon each other
in the city are —
wealth and poverty,
glamour and squalor,
bright lights and dark alleys,
hygienic wonders of glass,
steel and concrete
and crumbling
rat-infested slums.

There is tension in the city,
in the board-room, in the typing pool.
There is haste in the city,
in the office, in the street.
Shoulders jostle,
but rarely is there meeting.
People throng the city,
but loneliness is in their midst.

Pray for the needs concealed
behind the city's
mask of well-being.
Pray for:
 - The old-old young,
   with adventure already turned sour.
 - The desperate seekers after accommodation.
 - The pavement dwellers and the drop-outs.
 - The human jackals preying upon their fellows.
 - The decent, honest people, forever hurrying
   yet seldom asking where they are going.

It is in vain that you rise up early and go late to rest,
eating the bread of anxious toil;
Unless the Lord watches over the city,
the watchman stays awake in vain

(Psalm 127 RSV).

Prayer For The City

Lover of all,
Our cities are full of people who need you,
but how shall they learn that you care for them
and who shall tell of your presence
from the padlocked church in the city centre?

You raised up prophets
in the wilderness beyond Jordan;
raise up prophets
in the wilderness of our cities.
Equip us to keep watch with you
lest the stones cry out
that in this day,
we were the ones who strove in vain.

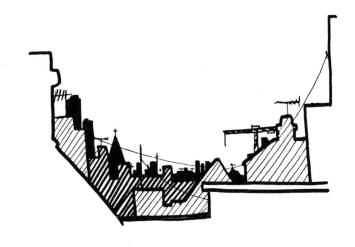

Freedom

5th after Pentecost

Yours was a world without hope and without God ... You are no longer aliens.
Ephesians 2.12,19 REB

You do not liberate me
by crying, 'God is dead'.
If it were true
there is no God,
and never was
except in our imagining;
should I rejoice
that all is ours
to do,
and then to die
as best we may?

May God forgive
the evil
practised in his name;
the superstitious fetters
forged from lack of faith;
the inability to trust
a love so great
that it enfolds
the whole created universe.

But, God be praised,
HE IS
and comes in Jesus Christ
as rescuer,
bridging in human life
the gulf between us
and our Maker.

You cannot set me free
from such a God.
HE is my freedom,
take me from HIM
and I become a slave.

Prayer Of A Sinner

6th after Pentecost

Ask, and you will receive; seek, and you will find; knock, and the door will be opened to you.

Matthew 7.7 REB

Repudiated Lord;
How can I come to you?
I acknowledge you with my lips
but I do not follow you with my feet.

Injured Lord;
How can I come to you?
I have lashed out in fear or bitterness
and in wounding those about me
have wounded you.

Crucified Lord;
How can I come to you?
In my arrogance and pride
I have declared your way unrealistic
and consented to your condemnation.

Risen Lord;
How can you come to me?
I acknowledge your resurrection
but have behaved as though it were
merely a matter of history.
I have not expected anything
in my own life to be changed . . .

Yet you do come,
breathing words of forgiveness,
of healing;
opening up
new dimensions of living.

Living Lord;
Forgive me what I am;
fill me, I pray, with your new life
and equip me to live in a way
which both
recognises
and reveals
your presence
in the everyday world
that you came to save.

The Human Face Of The Almighty

6th after Pentecost

But can God indeed dwell with mortals on earth?

2 Chronicles 6.18 REB

Jesus, we thank you
that in your earthly life
we have seen
the human face of the Almighty;
that from the immensity of the universe
we have heard the beating
of a human heart.

We thank you for your willingness
to share our concern for things,
that are trivial to others,
but tremendously important to us;
the things which make up so much
of our daily living.

We thank you for taking
our petty anxieties seriously
and for enriching simple occasions
with your presence.

As we live our lives day by day
help us to be so sure
of your loving concern
that we may be less worried
about what may happen
and more ready to live in the confidence
that all our ways
are always in your hands.

Love In Action

7th after Pentecost

Carry one another's burdens and in this way you will fulfil the law of Christ.
Galatians 6.2 REB

Lord, teach us to pray
as you would have us pray.
Save us from bringing
too many petitions,
and arouse in us instead
a desire to listen,
a desire to learn
your will for us.

Teach us to trust you,
not merely with the mind,
but in the commitment
of the whole of our being.

Teach us what it means
to pray for the sorrows of the world.
You have made those sorrows your own,
yet you still require disciples
to reach out in love
as the instruments of your caring.

We thank you for those men and women
in whom we have seen
something of the radiance
of that love in action.
May we learn from them
and
through your grace
working in us
show something
of the same love
in our own lives.

Before The Harvest

7th after Pentecost

I say you will recognise them by their fruit.

Matthew 7.20 REB

Before the harvest
the ripening,
before the ripening
the growing,
before the growing
the sowing,
before the sowing
the preparation of the soil.

**May we be so prepared
for the Spirit's sowing
that the seed
may grow in fruitful soil
and ripen to a worthy harvest.**

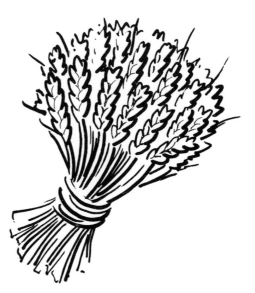

Fools For The Lord

8th after Pentecost

As God's ministers, we try to recommend ourselves in all circumstances by our steadfast endurance.

2 Corinthians 6.4 (but also see 1 – 10) REB

Fools, fools, fools for the Lord,
Laughed at and mocked,
Pushed to the side;
Fools, fools, fools for the Lord,
This is our calling,
This is our pride.

We are the liars who speak the truth,
We are the nobodies who all men know,
We are the dying who still live-on,
We are the victims who are not brought low,
Weak ourselves, we bring strength to other lives,
Impotent! We rule the world!

Fools, fools, fools for the Lord,
Laughed at and mocked,
Pushed to the side;
Fools, fools, fools for the Lord,
This is our calling,
This is our pride.

We are the innocent who stand condemned,
We are the criminals who do the right,
We are the atheists who worship God,
We are the helpless who rise up and fight;
Poor ourselves, we bring wealth to many souls,
Penniless! We own the world!

Fools, fools, fools for the Lord,
Laughed at and mocked,
Pushed to the side;
Fools, fools, fools for the Lord,
This is our calling,
This is our pride.

From *Ragman*

The Source Of Peace
(An Intercession)

8th after Pentecost *When you pass through water I shall be with you; when you pass through rivers they will not overwhelm you; walk through fire, and you will not be scorched, through flames and they will not burn you.*

Isaiah 43.2 – 3 REB

And thus it was that all came safely to land.

Acts 27.44 REB

Living Lord, in a dark hour you spoke of the gift of peace, we beg that gift for ourselves. Grant us, we pray, the inner serenity which you alone can give that we may become messengers of peace to a strife torn world.

>**Give peace in our time, O Lord.**
>**Give peace in our hearts, O Lord.**

We acknowledge that as Christians we are called to live as fully as we may, accepting with all life's delights its sufferings and its sorrows. We acknowledge that it is for us to offer dark and light alike to our heavenly Father who can weave even pain, grief, failure and defeat into his tapestry and make them glorious.

>**Give peace in our time, O Lord.**
>**Give peace in our hearts, O Lord.**

We pray for all who suffer for their fidelity to the calling to be your witnesses; all who suffer for trying to live by the truth they have received and all who are slandered, ill-treated, falsely imprisoned or tortured. Crucified and risen Lord, may they, sharing your anguish, know that they will also share your victory.

>**Give peace in our time. O Lord.**
>**Give peace in our hearts, O Lord.**

We pray for those who suffer as a result of the wickedness and folly of others. We especially pray for those who suffer from the breakdown of law and order, or from the absence of just and humane laws and are thus denied the freedom to realise their birthright as your children on this earth.

>**Give peace in our time, O Lord.**
>**Give peace in our hearts, O Lord.**

115

The Source of Peace
(An Intercession)

We pray for those who are fighting; injury, disfigurement, death their constant companions. Nerves and bodies strained beyond endurance, the streams of compassion drying up within them, their only goal the destruction of the 'enemy'.

Whatever the colour of their skin – we pray for them.
Whatever the sound of their tongue – we pray for them.
Whatever the insignia they wear – we pray for them.

>**Give peace in our time, O Lord.**
>**Give peace in our hearts, O Lord.**

We pray for all who have been broken in battle; for those who weep and for those who can no longer weep; for those who feel the anguish and for those who have lost the capacity to feel: for all prisoners and for all jailers; for those who exist in war torn lands and for those who no longer have a homeland.

>**Give peace in out time, O Lord.**
>**Give peace in our hearts, O Lord.**

We pray for those who stir up strife, for all who make a profit out of the misery of others, for all who are led into vice as they seek a momentary forgetfulness; and for all who believe that war is inevitable.

We bring to you particular needs . . .
And we remember those who have died . . .

Lord we pray that you may hold us fast amidst all the evils of this world, that at the last we may enter into the peace and joy of your kingdom.

>**Give peace in our time, O Lord.**
>**Give peace in our hearts, O Lord.**

Love, The Ultimate Weapon

9th after Pentecost

God was in Christ reconciling the world to himself, no longer holding people's misdeeds against them, and has entrusted us with the message of reconciliation.
2 Corinthians 5.19 REB

Almighty God,
you have created a universe so vast
that all our probings
only reveal the poverty of our knowledge.
You have created the atom,
invisible to the naked eye,
yet containing within it the restless energy
which we so fearfully and clumsily
work to release.
You are ever with us,
though your ways cannot be compassed
by the human mind.
We cannot escape from your presence
but neither can we possess or contain you
in any of our systems.

Yet, in a human life
you have made yourself known to us.
In spite of all our follies, all our sins,
you have reached out to us in Jesus.
Through him we learn
that the heart of the universe
is love, costly, sacrificial love;
holding nothing back
that we may be rescued
from death to life.

Help us, we pray,
to receive your love in Christ,
to make it our own.
Help us, that we may dare
to witness to love as the ultimate weapon.
Love willing to take pain to itself.
Love willing to be lost that others may be found.
Love willing to die that others may live.

Father God,
work your miracle in our hearts;
that we may share
in your work of reconciliation.

To Be Of The Kingdom

9th after Pentecost

Go and learn what this text means, 'I require mercy, not sacrifice. I did not come to call the virtuous, but sinners'.

Matthew 9.13 REB

Enable us, Lord Jesus,
to carry the reality of the Kingdom
deep in our hearts.
Save us from little-mindedness
and the fears
that would deny others
their part in the good things
given for all to enjoy.
Lead us in the ways of true fellowship
in our homes,
in our churches,
and in the world at large.

If I can reach the day
when there is:
 - No one towards whom I feel enmity.
 - No one I want to steal a march on.
 - No one I want to spite or put in their place.
 - No victory I want to win over others,
but only victories
with and for others.
Surely, Lord,
in that moment,
I shall have entered your Kingdom.

At The Lord's Table

10th after Pentecost

For the tradition which I handed on to you came to me from the Lord himself.
1 Corinthians 11.23 REB

When we break bread together
we share in the body of Christ;
each of us is part of the one body.
When we drink together in love,
we are renewed by the life of Christ,
given to each and everyone who seeks him.

> The eye cannot say to the hand,
> 'I do not need you'.
> Nor can the head say to the feet,
> 'I do not need you'. . .

Yet this is exactly
what we do.
At the very Table
where Christ
would make us one
we are divided.

We are so scrupulous,
so fearful we may lose
something precious,
that Christ's body remains broken,
his church divided.

> **Saviour Christ,**
> **as we share again**
> **the bread of life,**
> **enlarge our understanding,**
> **teach us what it means**
> **to love one another**
> **as you love us,**
> **and make us one,**
> **that the world may believe.**

The Open Door Of The Church

10th after Pentecost

As you go proclaim the message: 'The kingdom of Heaven is upon you.'
Matthew 10.7 REB

Thank you, Lord,
for the open door of the Church;
open that we may enter,
be welcome
and find in fellowship
the renewal of our spirits.

And thank you, Lord,
for the closed door of the Church;
shutting behind us
as we go out into the world
of daily living;
the closed door which cries,
'Not here, but risen,
and gone ahead of you.'

Too easily we forget
what it means
to live in the age of the Resurrection;
and so we pray,
when all seems dark,
and we are inclined to feel sorry for ourselves
and hide with our memories in the Upper Room,
meet with us
and call us out again,
to where there are battles
to be fought
and lost —
and won!

Like A Child

11th after Pentecost

Whoever does not accept the kingdom of God like a child will never enter it.
Mark 10.15 REB

You said we must become
as little children
if we would see the Kingdom of Heaven;
but it was when we were children
that we first discovered
how painful it is to be vulnerable,
and we began to build defences
around our hearts
against hurt.

As the years have passed
those defences have grown thicker,
irregular,
makeshift,
but sufficient to dull the impact
of some of life's blows;
sufficient to hide the nakedness
of our hopes,
our dreams,
our ideals
and we have come to depend upon them.

And you tell us we must become again
as little children;
trusting,
as open to hurt as an infant.

Is the refusal to be vulnerable a sin?
In building our defences against the world,
setting limits on our giving,
caring,
loving;
are we buildings barriers
against the life of the Kingdom?

> **Lord, help us;**
> **strengthen us that we may dare**
> **to put our security in your hands,**
> **dare to be vulnerable,**
> **that,**
> **rediscovering childlike trust**
> **we may find ourselves at home**
> **in your Kingdom.**

Nothing Is Greater Than Love

11th after Pentecost

When we love God and obey his commands we love his children too.
1 John 5.2 REB

Can you imagine
Just one thing
That will fill you
With all the joy of living?
Can you imagine
Just one thing
You can give,
But be richer for the giving?

Love knows no limit to its patience and its caring,
Love, ever trusting, is adventurous and daring,
Love is of God and its power grows with sharing,
Nothing is greater than love.

Can you imagine
Just one thing,
Something vast,
And which flows through all creation?
Can you imagine
Just one thing
That is free
As a gift to ever nation?

Love is a force that is steadily advancing,
Love is a joy you will always find entrancing,
Love is a liberty that sets your spirit dancing,
Nothing is greater than love.

Can you imagine
Just one thing
That looks weak,
Though there's nothing quite so strong?
Can you imagine
Just one thing
That will last
When all other things have gone?

Love knows no limit to the service it is giving
Love will take knocks, but it never stops forgiving,
Love is of God, it's the only way of living,
Nothing is greater than love.

From *Ragman.*

122

Fools Gold?

12th after Pentecost

A pure and faultless religion in the sight of God the Father is this: to look after orphans and widows in trouble and to keep oneself untarnished by the world.
James 1.27 REB

The worker in precious metals
will not be deceived by fools' gold;
shall we show less discrimination
and acclaim as precious
the faith that is no faith?

The faith that is no faith
commits to God
the cause of the orphan, widow, homeless,
the despairing and the desperate;
lays at the feet of the Almighty
in earnest prayer
the sorrows of the world,
trusts him to set them right
and goes home satisfied
to supper and to bed.

True faith
is fashioned from another mould.
It sees the sorrows of the world
a burden all too great
for God to bear alone;
sees God bowed down,
staggering to Calvary,
grateful that Simon of Cyrene
should put his shoulder beneath the cross.

True faith
believes that God makes
each human need his own,
yet waits on human minds
to catch his thoughts
and turn those thoughts to deeds.

True faith
lays at the feet of the Almighty
in earnest prayer
the sorrows of the world,
prays to have some part in meeting them
and goes out
seeking opportunity.

Fool's Gold

Teach us to pray, Lord
as those who
desire to listen,
desire to learn your will
and desire your grace
to help them to do it.

Teach us how to trust you
not merely with the mind,
but in the commitment
of the whole of our being.

Teach us to pray
for the sorrows of the world,   *tack of this day*
as those who know
that you have made
those sorrows your own
and yet require disciples
to reach out in loving compassion
as the instruments of your care.

We thank you for those
who are radiant channels of your love,
help us to learn from them.
Inspire and strengthen us
that we may be numbered
amongst them
and faithfully do
whatever work it is
that you put into our hands.

Help Us As We Hesitate

12th after Pentecost

You must be made new in mind and spirit.

Ephesians 4.23 NEB

To do this
or to do that?
To go here,
or not go there?
Each day we must make decisions,
so many decisions
that sometimes the things that really matter,
the really big issues,
get crowded out.

Bring us back, Lord,
when we get our priorities all wrong;
bring us back
to the heart of the matter.
Remind us that nothing is more important
than that we should be doing
the work you have assigned to us.

Help us to ask what,
in love,
you would have us do today
and tomorrow
and the tomorrow after that.
And when we get caught up in trivialities,
as we do,
bring us back again
to the same question.

> **Love
> from the heart of God,
> surround us and fill us.
> Strength
> from the heart of God,
> stiffen our will.
> Purpose
> from the heart of God,
> be the meaning of our living,
> now and for ever.**

And Afterwards?

13th after Pentecost

Go; do not sin again.

John 8.11 REB
(But see also verses 1 – 11)

It is but a fragment
of a story . . .

Who was she,
this woman
brought to Jesus
scared out of her wits?
And who were her accusers,
outraged relatives,
husband,
brothers,
father even;
eager for her death?

And
What happened afterwards?
They went away
O yes,
they went away,
and she was left.
Their outraged male pride
had been rebuked
but had their anger died?
Dare she
ever again
go home
and face them?

Or
Was there a family
among the friends of Jesus
who took her in
to help her rebuild
her shattered life?

> **Lord, your mercy shames us,**
> **but also, we pray,**
> **stir us,**
> **when you need us**
> **to give practical support**
> **to ones you would redeem.**

Our Greater Need

13th after Pentecost

Through the body of Christ you died to the law and were set free to give yourselves . . . to him who rose from the dead so that we may bear fruit for God.
Romans 7.4 REB

Lord, when we come to you in prayer
all too often
our first instinct
is to pour out
all our troubles and worries
and implore your help.

We know you hear us,
yet the longer
we are with you
the more we begin to recognize
that our greater need
is for help
in the inner battle of the soul,
lest the enemy find us
utterly unprepared
and defenceless.

Sinners that we are,
you died for us.
Forgive our blindness,
our prejudice
and our self-centredness.
Forgive us that much of our striving
has little to do with your kingdom.
Forgive us that all too often
when you call us to service
we offer little but excuses.

Lord, let the warmth of your love
so flood our hearts
that it may melt
the ice that grips them
and save us into life.

Make Us Aware

14th after Pentecost

Take great care, then, how you behave: act sensibly, not like simpletons . . . for these are evil days.

part of Ephesians 5.15 – 16 REB

Save us from the great sins,
the named sins,
the sins that decent men and women
recognise and shun;
But save us also from the subtle grip of other sins,
sins that we easily excuse and camouflage and justify.

We laugh at the idea of
'Keeping up with the Jones',
but we do not want our house
to be less well furnished
than the houses of our friends
or our car to be shabbier than theirs.
We try to keep abreast
of steadily rising living standards
and think ourselves hard done by
that we still have unsatisfied desires.

Save us from contentment
with being no worse than others.
Save us from conveniently deaf ears and blind eyes.
Save us from sins of self-interest and self indulgence.

Save us from sins
that wear a cloak of virtue or necessity.
Save us from offering excuses
when we should be offering ourselves.
Save us from calling light darkness
and darkness light.

We ask that you will help us
when we pray
to listen rather than to talk.
We ask that you will help us
as we seek the way ahead
to recognize the work to which you are pointing.
Lord help us to live
fully, freely and joyously
alive with you all our days.

Prayer Of A Wayfarer

**14th
after
Pentecost**

And now I will show you the best way of all.

1 Corinthians 13.1 NEB
(But see also verses 1 – 13)

I am ashamed
that I have travelled so little distance
in the way of love.
I hear again the words

‘Love is patient’.

Sometimes
when people need me to be around
a part of me,
with restless impatience,
is wondering how soon I can get away.
Forgive me my lack of patience.

‘Love is kind and envies no one.’

I don’t always find it easy
when others are on top of the world
and want me to share their delight;
especially if I have had a set-back
or been hurt.
Forgive me when I am mean or envious.

‘Love is never boastful, nor conceited, nor rude.’

But the urge to contend
is strong in me.
When I push myself forward
and strive for ascendancy over others,
forgive me my self assertion.

‘Love is never selfish, nor quick to take offence.’

Lord, forgive me when I am intolerant,
touchy, too bound up in myself,
for with all the cause I have given you
to be offended
you have never turned from me.

Prayer Of A Wayfarer

'Love keeps no score of wrongs, does not gloat over
other men's sins, but delights in the truth.'

Save me
from tabulating the failings of others,
but save me also
from being indifferent to evil
and teach me to delight in the truth.

'There is nothing love cannot face, there is no limit
to its faith, its hope, its endurance. Love will
never come to an end.'

Lord, I know I could never love like that,
but I do believe that such a love
is reaching out to me;
let your love so flow in me and through me,
let it so possess me,
that I may travel at least a few steps further
in the best way of all.

Ready To Be Disciples

15th after Pentecost

No one who does not carry his cross and come with me can be a disciple of mine.
Luke 14.27 REB

Lord Jesus,
there are no words adequate
to respond to your
giving of yourself to us.
You carry the burden
of our follies,
our weaknesses
and our wilful sins.
You know us through and through
and you are constantly
being wounded by us,
yet you still care,
you still love us.

We are poor disciples.
We declare our loyalty
but then fail
to follow where you lead.
Unflinchingly
you trod the way of love;
we are liable to hesitate
at every step.
We fear the pain
and the suffering
which love can bring,
yet deep in our hearts
we know that your way
is the true way to life.

Lord, forgive us what we are
and help us to become
what you would have us be.

The Unity Of The Church

Surely Christ has not been divided!

1 Corinthians 1.13 REB

Lord Jesus,
we would pray for the church
which is one
in the greatness of your love,
but divided
in the littleness of our own.
May we be less occupied
with the things
which divide us,
and realise more
that which
we hold in common.
As wise men
and shepherds
were both drawn
to your manger;
so may we become
one family
in you
who has called us all
from darkness
into
the light of life.

The Medium Is The Message?

16th after Pentecost

Let the message of Christ dwell among you in all its richness.
Colossians 3.16 NEB

Was he a good man?
A truly good man?
To many
Jesus
was a law-breaker,
and a blasphemer;
they didn't think him good.
He turned accepted standards
upside down.

Men and women stood aghast
that he cared
so little
for ecclesiastical rules and traditions;
that he cared
so much
for the outcast, the despised;
for the man whose business ethics
were unacceptable;
for the woman who sold herself
as a momentary substitute for love.

The medium is not always the message,
yet medium and message were one in him.
The question,
'Was he a good man?'
becomes irrelevant;
he overset the existing order
and good became what he was.

To this day it is not a rule
but an experience;
not a code for living
but a life;
not words,
however carefully they may be chosen,
but
THE WORD MADE FLESH,
medium and message in one.

Why This Waste?

16th after Pentecost

Jesus was at Bethany, in the house of Simon the leper. As he sat at table, a woman came in carrying a bottle of very costly perfume, pure oil of nard. She broke it open and poured the oil over his head.

Mark 14.3 REB

They were horrified!
The whole room
was absolutely horrified,
but it was done
before anyone
could stop her.
And not just a few drops,
delicately placed behind the ears,
but the whole flask!
For heaven's sake,
the whole flask
of such a perfume
as would have been
welcomed in palaces,
poured on the head
of one whose life style
was simplicity itself.

How unfortunate that this
obviously unbalanced woman
should appear
and embarrass him
with such an impulsive
extravagant gesture.
Wherever did she get the flask?
Look what money
it would have fetched
in the market . . .

'Leave her alone.' he said,
'Why make trouble for her?
It is a fine thing
she has done for me.'

> Lord, we know that we should exercise
> a proper stewardship of all our resources;
> help us to do this;
> but help us also to recognize
> the moments
> when all rules may be overset
> at the impulse of a loving heart.

134

What Does Love Demand?

17th after Pentecost

As God's dear children, you must be like him. Live in love as Christ loved you.

part of Ephesians 5.1 – 2 REB

Before ever it receives
the Queen's Assent
and reaches the Statute Book,
each new Act of Parliament
will have been scrutinized by lawyers
eager to defy the spirit
whilst honouring the letter.

Where the law touches them
many citizens will do the same.
The payment of tax
can become a contest
between Inspector
and taxpayer
whose bible
is *Money Which?*
and whose prophet
is his accountant.

The State defines the bounds,
and citizens
in their own interests
may push those bounds
to the very limit
that the law permits.

But that is not the way of the Kingdom.
The law of the Kingdom
knows nothing
of subtle interpretation
of clause
and sub-clause,
for the whole law is comprehended
in three words,
'You shall love!'.

'Where does the advantage lie?'
is a question
quite unknown within the Kingdom;

What Does Love Demand?

there the question asked
of each new situation is,
'What does love demand?'

Love
that derives from him
who,
living by the law of love,
went to a cross
and cried,
'Father forgive them:
they do not know what they are doing'.

> **Help us, we pray,**
> **to live,**
> **less by the law**
> **of cherished rights,**
> **and more by the law**
> **of unlimited responsibility.**
> **Teach us to love,**
> **and loving,**
> **to love**
> **with all our might.**

Prayer For The Family
(An Intercession)

17th after Pentecost

I kneel in prayer to the Father, from whom every family in heaven and on earth takes its name.

Ephesians 3.14 – 15 REB

Father God, you have so made us
that we depend upon one another;
we all need other human beings
and others in turn need us.
To be complete people
we must love and be loved.

Forgive us our sins against our families;
the times when we take our homes for granted,
the times when we are blind to weariness or pain
in others in the household,
the times when we too readily assume
that what suits us will suit others also.
Forgive us when we give too little
and expect too much.

We pray for the very young
that they may be surrounded by such loving care
and guidance as gives them room to grow,
unfettered, but secure.
As the years pass may they find rich experiences
in an ever widening world
whilst still enjoying and being supported by
their families.

We pray for young men and women
as they begin to make their own homes;
may they retain joyous roots
in the homes that gave them birth.

We pray for young parents
that they may find an additional dimension of happiness
in the new life given into their care;
and for grandparents,
that they may enjoy their grandchildren
so that young and old
may enrich each other's living.

Prayer For The Famiy
(An Intercession)

We pray for the elderly, aware of failing powers,
for the sick,
and all those challenged by disability,
that they may find support,
for they too have a contribution to make
in the family.

Finally we pray for those
who know no family life;
may overflowing love provide for them
families which accept them to themselves,
where they can love and be loved
and find the joy of personal relationships
which is your will for us all.

You Won't Believe It!

18th after Pentecost

'If they do not listen to Moses and the prophets they will pay no heed even if someone should rise from the dead.'

Luke 16.31 REB

And so he came
to judgement.

Being a thoroughly modern
sophisticated person
he hadn't believed in an after-life.
His burial, with all the honours
befitting his wealth and rank;
followed by a costly memorial
testifying to his many accomplishments,
should have been
the end of the story.

Instead, he came to judgement
and was found wanting.
Even so, he could not abandon
the habits of a lifetime.

'Send Lazarus:'
    – He knew his name,
    the beggar
    who had waited at his door.
'Send Lazarus to help me.'

It couldn't be.

'Then at least send Lazarus
to warn my brothers.'
The answer came, 'They, also
were trained in the laws of God.
If they have rejected compassion;
if their hearts are flint;
they will pay no heed
even though someone
should rise from
the dead.'

So Much Yet So Little

18th after Pentecost

You yourselves were alienated from God . . . But now by Christ's death in his body of flesh and blood God has reconciled you to himself.
                                        part of Colossians 1.21 – 22 REB

Lord Jesus,
we have so much,
yet at the same time
we have so little.
All too often
we strive after the riches
of this world
as if they were
the only reality.

Save us, we pray
from building our lives
upon this
insecure foundation.
Save us
from falling
into the snares
laid for us by Mammon.

Help us, we pray
to know your living presence
Let our lives
be transformed
by your life within us.
Teach us to be
more loving,
more caring;
saved
by your death,
witnesses
to your resurrection.

That We May See The Glory

19th after Pentecost

If their thoughts had been with the country they had left, they could have found opportunity to return. Instead we find them longing for a better country, a heavenly one. That is why God is not ashamed to be called their God; for he has a city ready for them.

Hebrews 11.15 – 16 REB

But that city
is still far off,
and in every one of us
there is a battle
between darkness and light.
Sometimes the light burns very low
and the darkness
appears to be impenetrable.

> **Break through the darkness that surrounds us, O Lord,
> and teach us to walk by the light of your glory.**

We pray for all in the grip of darkness;
the darkness of fear,
of despair,
of ignorance;
the darkness of a self-centred life;
the darkness of a sense of failure.

> **Break through the darkness that surrounds us, O Lord,
> and teach us to walk in the light of your glory.**

Lord, we have faith,
help us where faith falls short.
Lord, there is a spark
of your fire within us,
fan it into a flame;
help us to share
with men and women everywhere
the vision of the city
which has no need of moon or sun,
where the glory of God
gives light,
and where all
may dwell together in peace.

> **Break through the darkness that surrounds us, O Lord,
> and teach us to walk by the light of your glory.**

Renewal

19th after Pentecost

For we must all have our lives laid open before the tribunal of Christ.
part of 2 Corinthians 5.10 REB

Lord Jesus,
you know so much better
than we do ourselves,
just how much our lives are disfigured by sin;
just how much our desires and dreams
are twisted and distorted;
and yet you still reach out to us.

The more we are aware of your presence
the more we are appalled
by what we see in ourselves.
It is your love alone
that gives us cause for hope.
Despite our dulled senses
you find ways to stir our hearts;
you accept us as we are
whilst awakening us to
what we should be:
you call us to trust ourselves
to your utter dependability
and so to discover our peace.

Lord, by your poverty
you make us rich;
out of your weakness
we renew our strength;
and by your dying
we are brought to life.

Pay Caesar What Is Due To Caesar

20th after Pentecost

Discharge your obligations to everyone; pay tax and levy, reverence and respect, to those to whom they are due.

Romans 13.7 REB

Then pay to Caesar what belongs to Caesar, and to God what belongs to God.
Matthew 22.21 REB

Is Christian living, then,
merely a matter of being
a model conformist citizen
who never rocks the boat;
pays taxes on the nail;
saves –
or spends –
as the times require,
watches Ministerial broadcasts,
queues patiently in the Post Office
and never parks on a double yellow line?

'Pay Caesar what belongs to Caesar,
and God what belongs to God'.
Jesus put the two together
and was executed
by Caesar's government.
And so was Paul,
and Peter,
and a line of martyrs
stretching
to this very day.

All have duties as citizens.
All have obligations
to the human community;
yet if the state demands
that to which
the state has no right,
the Christian must witness
to higher loyalties;
that Caesar
and Caesar's household
may know that they also
are under authority.

Pay Caesar What Is Due To Caesar
(An Intercession)

20th after Pentecost

I have taught you statutes and laws, as the Lord my God commanded me; see that you keep them . . .

part of Deuteronomy 4.5 REB

Source of all justice and truth
you have given us the ability
to know good from evil
and you call us to live
by your laws.

We pray for our nation
and for those who have responsibility
for guiding and governing in our land.

We pray for
      our Queen and all the members of the Royal Family,
      elected representatives of the people,
      government and local government officials,
      those involved in the administration of the law,
      those who shape and direct our trade and industry,
      all engaged in education
      and in health and welfare services.

With all our hearts we pray for the peace of the realm;
      for peace grounded in justice,
      peace arising out of a striving for true community.
      We pray that as a people
      we may have proper care for the weak
      and the impoverished;
      acknowledging that every human being
      has rights
      as a child
      of the Living God.

We pray that we may at all times
be worthy and responsible citizens;
but if ever the day should come
when we are charged with breaking our country's laws,
may it not be for failure to live responsibly,
but for being witnesses to a kingdom
whose claims are above all other.

144

In A Time Of Crisis
(An Intercession)

21st after Pentecost

They were all trying to intimidate us, in the hope that we should then relax our efforts and that the work would never be completed. Strengthen me for the work, was my prayer.

Nehemiah 6.9 REB

Lord Jesus,
You accept and value us just as we are.
Do not let our feelings of weakness or disability,
our fear of the frailties of age,
our bitterness or resentment
mar the lives we offer you.

Forgive us when we fail to live
as fully as we might.
Forgive us when we think more
of our disabilities than our possibilities.
Forgive us, Lord, we pray,
and make us whole.

We pray for the fellowship of the church
into which you have called us.
You call us to be loving, caring people,
putting the needs of others before our own,
reflecting your way of life in the world.
Often we fail you.

We fail you through fear,
through shortsightedness,
and through sheer lack of faith
that your way really does work.
Forgive us, Lord, we pray,
and make our fellowship whole.

We pray for men and women in the wider world,
including those who never pray for themselves.
 For those weighed down by sickness and disability.
 For those suffering prolonged pain.
 For those who feel isolated and lonely.
 For those who are conscious
 of having made a mess of their lives.
 And for all who long for healing of body,
 mind and spirit.

145

In A Time Of Crisis
(An Intercession)

Lord, we know your love reaches out
to all your children
Help each and every one of us
to be more aware of that love,
that we may be able to receive it,
make it our own
and through it be renewed
for whatever work
you have for us to do.

The Buried Talent

21st after Pentecost

I was afraid, and went and hid thy talent in the earth.

Matthew 25.25 AV
(But see also verses 14 – 30)

Welcome home, master,
it's nice to see you back,
the place isn't the same without you;
I hope you had a good trip . . .

The talent you entrusted to me?
Yes, master,
I was just coming to that.
It worried me of course,
not knowing what to do for the best.
You are so great,
so powerful,
and if I may say so,
so shrewd,
that everything you touch prospers;
now how could I compete with that?

Yes, I know the others traded
and made a handsome profit,
just like you do —
and good luck to them, I say;
but I'm not in that league;
I know my limitations.

What if I'd traded and lost,
what would you have said then?
And anyway,
when you gave me less
than you gave the others
I knew you didn't expect much of me.

'No', I said to myself,
'the best thing I can do
is to give him his stake back
just as he gave it to me.'
And here it is.
I apologize if the coins
are a bit tarnished,
but the safe place where I buried them
turned out to be a little damp.

147

The Buried Talent

The master replies —

So you've brought your stake back,
unused, tarnished;
What do you expect me to say to that?
You call me master,
you say that you know my ways,
know that I take risks:
then wasn't it your duty
to follow where I lead
and yourself take risks in my service?

I grant you had less than the others,
But you had something
well within your capacity to manage
and did nothing with it;
you didn't even try.

What more can I do with you?
If you won't even
make an effort
to follow my ways
I have no choice
but to pass your work
to another.

Losing And Winning

22nd after Pentecost

Stephen, filled with the Holy Spirit, and gazing intently up to heaven, saw the glory of God, and Jesus standing at God's right hand.

Acts 7.55 REB

O lord of the Kingdom
Where losing is winning
And love has a strength which
Gives promise of dawn;
Teach us in our doubting
to know resurrection
And live in your world as
A people reborn.

O joy of the sinner
And hope of the dying,
O peace of the troubled,
Lord, help us we pray;
Banish now the sorrow,
The death which enfolds us,
Forgive us, renew us,
Restore us today.

O living Lord Jesus
We share in your triumph,
The world may be dark but
we live by your word;
Death has no dominion
For Jesus is risen.
Away with our grieving,
Rejoice in the Lord.

O Lord in your kingdom
The poorest is welcome,
The homeless find lodging,
the outcast belong;
Fill us with your loving
And free us Lord Jesus
to worship and serve you
All ages along.

By What Authority?

22nd after Pentecost

'Tell us,' they said, 'by what authority you are acting like this; who gave you this authority?'

Luke 20.2 REB

We naturally expect the bus driver,
the train driver, the ship's captain
or the aircraft pilot,
to be fully trained
and qualified.

So with doctors, dentists, lawyers,
police officers, architects and builders,
accountants, and an ever growing list
of public servants:
we rightly expect
training and authentication
by some recognized body.

In the churches,
that all may be done
decently and in order,
we carefully select, train
and set aside by ordination our ministers.

Yet the Lord of the Church
was not trained or authenticated
by any recognized body.
His authority came from within,
sealed by his death and resurrection.

> **O Lord our God,**
> **you often speak to your people**
> **through unlikely messengers**
> **and in unexpected ways.**
> **Give us, we pray,**
> **the wisdom to recognize**
> **and the humility to receive**
> **your word**
> **through whatever person**
> **and in whatever manner**
> **it may come to us.**

The Race

Last after Pentecost

We too must throw off every encumbrance and the sin that all too easily restricts us, and run with resolution the race which lies ahead of us.
Hebrews 12.1 REB

Winning and losing
take on new meaning
in the race which lies ahead of us,
for each entrant
has a route
which is theirs alone.

It is not a sprint,
all effort concentrated
in a few vital seconds;
nor is it run
on a prepared and measured track,
but cross country,
the ground unknown,
the weather unpredictable.
there could be long uneventful stretches
but the going can also
become mighty rough.

It may lead
through town or countryside,
sunshine or storm,
joys or agony
until . . .

The climax
may be long foreseen
or it may take us by surprise.
We may think
we have hardly started,
or
– having stepped aside
to help another runner –
that we have lost our way.

Suddenly we are in the stadium,
there is a sea of faces,
runners who completed the course before us,
faces we know.
The race is run,
we are home.

The Eternal Kingdom

Last after Pentecost

I press towards the finishing line, to win the heavenly prize to which God has called me in Christ Jesus.

Philippians 3.14 REB

Almighty and everlasting God,
you are all in all,
yet you have made yourself known to us
through our Lord Jesus Christ.
In him you have entered into
all the limitations
and disappointments
of human living.
In him you make our sorrows your own,
contend with the powers
of sin and of death,
and enable us to share
in Christ's resurrection.

We praise you for
giving us purpose and goal
for our ambitions and hopes.

We praise you for
turning words like success and failure
inside out
and the judgements of the world
upside down.

We praise you that
even as we live in this world
we may be citizens of heaven,
and our lives
may find their fulfilment
in the service of your kingdom.

We praise you for
your faithful witnesses
of this age and every age,
of this land and every land;
women and men,
old and young,
known and unknown,
statesman and labourer,
artisan and scholar.

The Eternal Kingdom

We praise you for
all your saints and martyrs,
drawn from every people
and from every age.

We praise you for their fidelity
to the truth they knew,
for their fortitude in meeting suffering,
for their witness to the Lord they served.

We pray that we may so live
our lives on earth
that we may be numbered amongst
your servants
and enter at the last
into the joy of your eternal kingdom.

The Good Earth

Harvest

Now I have brought here the first fruits of the soil which you Lord, have given me.

Deuteronomy 26.10 REB

Glory be to God
who has created all that we see
and all that lies beyond our seeing.
Glory be to God
who has created all that we know
and all that lies beyond our knowing.
Glory be to God
who holds in his loving care
all that our minds can conceive
and all that lies beyond our conceiving.

Father, we thank you for the beauty
and the fruitfulness of the land
in which we live.
We thank you for the wide variety
of the world's harvests and the riches
from other countries which we enjoy.
We thank you that we need never
go hungry or thirsty, not knowing
where to turn for food or drink.

Save us from taking these many gifts
for granted.
Stimulate our concern for your needy peoples
who starve in a world of plenty.
Guide us that we may be stewards,
not squanderers of your creation.

Forgive us the damage we have done,
knowingly or unknowingly, through the destruction
or pollution of our environment.
Forgive us the harm we have done,
knowingly or unknowingly, to other creatures
you have made to share in the life of this planet.
Forgive us the ill we have done,
knowingly or unknowingly, to other human beings,
our brothers and sisters in Christ.

154

The Good Earth

Father, the riches we enjoy
come from you,
given freely to us all.
Stir us to open our hearts
and giving as freely as we have received,
to joyfully share our blessings with others.

Blessed Be The Name Of The Lord

Harvest

While the earth remaineth, seedtime and harvest, and cold and heat, and summer and winter, and day and night, shall not cease.

Genesis 8.22 AV

O the grain in the hand
Became the seed in the soil,
And the seed in the soil
Became the shoot in the field,
And the shoot in the field
Became the stalk waving green,
And the stalk waving green
Became the corn golden brown,
And the corn golden brown
Became the grain in the barn,
And the grain in the barn
Became the bread that we eat;
Blessed be the name of the Lord,
Blessed be the name of the Lord.

For the Lord has promised
While the earth remains,
There'll be time for planting
And a time to reap,
There'll be cold days and hot days,
Dry days and wet days,
Winter and summer,
Darkness and light;
This is the Word
That the Lord has spoken:
This is the Word
That the Lord has spoken:
Blessed be the name of the Lord,
Blessed be the name of the Lord.

From *The Alien*, a musical play based on the story of Ruth.

Index by Subject

Affirmation of faith 84
Authority 150

Beatitudes 54

Christ
 – and the marginalized 25, 31, 58, 96, 99,
   101, 126, 133, 134, 149
 – his body 76, 119, 131
 – his passion and crucifixion 70, 73, 74, 76,
   78, 79
 – his resurrection 80, 81, 82, 83, 85, 86, 91,
   92
 – his way 70, 88, 125, 132, 140
Church, and the world 46, 61, 98, 99, 100,
   101, 120
City life 34, 58, 69, 73, 74, 78, 117
Creation 9, 154, 156

Darkness and light 141, 156
Difficult times 22, 23, 25, 28, 29, 31, 43, 99
Doing nothing 147

Easter 80, 81, 82, 83, 85, 86, 91, 92
Everyday living 40, 46, 69, 154
Extravagance 134

Facing
 – disaster 13, 14
 – temptation 12, 40, 62, 63, 79
Faith 119
Family life 35, 37, 137
Freedom 19, 25, 47, 57, 109, 149

God
 – armour of 64
 – authorized by 150
 – chosen by 15, 17, 19, 20, 43, 66, 67, 70
 – human experience of 94, 112
 – kingdom of 45, 62, 101, 118, 120, 121,
   135, 141, 144, 149, 152
 – seeking 38, 110
 – without 109
Good and evil 11, 12, 64

Harvest 9, 13, 14, 59, 89, 113, 154, 156
Homelessness 101, 107
Hope 13, 73, 141, 142

Human nature 10
Humble service 69, 76, 114

Incarnation 33, 34, 35, 44, 48, 117, 133
Injustice 30, 101, 139, 147
Intercession 50, 63, 71, 92, 96, 115, 137, 145

Learning
 – to pray 16, 110, 112
 – wisdom 11, 21, 38, 54, 56
Love 11, 21, 38, 54, 56
 – costly 34, 58, 69, 73, 74, 78, 118
 – security of 61, 71
 – supremacy of 122, 125, 129, 135
Loneliness 22, 120

Miracles 44, 48, 57, 58, 59

New Life 86

Old age 36, 137

Pain and suffering 71, 78
Peace 115
Pressure 90, 104

Rectitude 134
Renewal 29, 41, 85, 86, 119, 142
Riches 53, 123, 140

Sabbath 52
Salvation 103
Scripture, the word 27, 32, 33, 133, 150
Simple things 33, 35, 48, 53, 83, 111
Speech which divides 95
Spirit
 – gifts of 89, 96, 100, 113
 – emptiness 85, 140

Unity 98, 100, 104

Visions
 – uncomfortable 17, 19, 68
Vulnerability 66, 71, 114, 121

Water of life 105, 106
Whole people 145
Winning and losing 81, 149, 151

Index of First Lines

A leper has no friends	58
A meeting during a journey	83
Across the ages two cries conflicting	73
Adam blamed Eve	40
Alarm bells ring!	13
Almighty God, you have created a universe so vast	117
Almighty and everlasting God	152
And so he came to judgement	139
Angel or tempter?	62
Beggarman, beggarman, born in a stable	34
Before the harvest	113
Before ever it receives the Queen's Assent	135
Beneath and outward calm	12
Being sensible men and women, Lord	66
But that city is still far off,	141
Can news ever be good for everybody?	23
Can you imagine just one thing	122
Climbing the stairs to that Upper Room	76
Coat of mail, helmet, shield and sword	65
Creator God, you have made us	52
Crucified and risen Lord, we pray	92
Dietrich Bonhoeffer was executed	71
Do we not share the anxiety	37
Doctors! Faith healers!	57
Enable us, Lord Jesus	118
Father God, you have so made us	137
Father, we fear that we often	16
Father, why are we such restless creatures	21
'Feed my sheep', you said	87
Fools, fools, fools for the Lord	114
Glory be to God	154
God is not like me	10
He read from a scroll of the prophet Isaiah	25
He stood before the court	30
Help us, Lord, for you have faced temptation	63
Helpless, he hung spreadeagled	78
Here we are, Lord, quietly bowed in prayer	50
I am ashamed that I have travelled	129
'I am the way.' But not for the unthinking	88
I may leave the Bible neatly shelved	32
If I can reach the day	118
If only the devil would appear	62
In the all-too familiar wilderness	17
Is Christian living, then, merely a matter	143
Is there something wrong with our prayers, Lord?	28
It is but a fragment of a story	126
It isn't easy to recognise	43
It was impossible! Beyond hope	81
It was no easy calling	42
It was unobtrusive, The Coming	48
Jesus, Teacher and Saviour	56
Jesus, we thank you	111
Kingdom coming, Kingdom present	45
Life now! That you come not merely	86
Like the summer of our youth	100
Living Lord, in a dark hour	115
Lord, as I face the passing of the years	36
Lord, as we face both the major difficulties	104
Lord, I know that you are risen	85
Lord, it would be so much easier	20
Lord Jesus, there are no words adequate	131
Lord Jesus, we have so much	140
Lord Jesus, we would pray for the church	132
Lord Jesus, when you entered Jerusalem	74
Lord Jesus, you accept and value us	145
Lord Jesus, you know so much better	142
Lord Jesus, you went to John	41
Lord of the ages	14
Lord of the outcast and the dispossessed	101
Lord, Saviour; we thank you	61
Lord, teach us to pray	112
Lord, we bring you our love	46
Lord, when we come to you in prayer	127
Lost to sight in the clouds!	94
Mary Magdalene speaks	79
Mary Magdalene speaks	80
Nine gifts, yet one	89
'No other name!'	103
O crucified and risen Lord	91
O God, where shall I go, what shall I do?	80
O Lord of the kingdom	149
O grain in the hand	156

Index of First Lines

Origin and life of the Universe   39

Pressing in upon each other   107

Quiet puss! Someone's at the door   22

Repudiated Lord; how can I come
to you?   110

Save us from the great sins   128
Saviour Lord, if ever we are to be
the means   19
Slowly he wheels his barrow of dead
leaves   64
Source of all justice and truth   144
Source of our deepest longings   38
Spirit of power, we find it hard   96
Sprechen Sie Deutsch?   95

Thank you, Lord, for the open door   120
The heavens tell out the glory of God   9
The moment of vision can be shattering   68
The road Christ trod is not listed by
the AA   70
The worker in precious metals   123
There was a wedding in Cana-in-Galilee   44
They used to say I had seven devils   79
They were horrified!   134
This I believe, that you are true   84
To do this or to do that?   125
To walk among lonely hills   53

Was he a good man?   133
We are thirsty!   105

We come to you, the human Christ   68
We confess, Lord, that we are not
the people   29
We confess with shame   98
We constantly discover new needs   54
We easily forget, but, long long
afterwards   59
We have sisters and brothers under
pressure   90
We must not be misled by the sheer poetic
beauty   33
We naturally expect the bus driver   150
We rejoice that you are a God who
breaks into history   99
We thank you, Lord, for all the ways   35
We thank you our God and Father   27
Welcome home, master   147
What can we say, Lord?   31
When the springs of my life run dry   106
When we break bread together   119
Whenever we begin to take you
seriously   69
'Who's there?' Starting at every sound   82
Why should one be called and not
another   15
Winning and losing take on new
meaning   151

You are the source of all knowledge   11
You do not liberate me   109
You call us to step out into the unknown   67
You said we must become as little
children   121
Young, healthy, educated, ambitious   47